MW01168339

CAUGHT

BETWEEN

COMING AND GOING

By

ROBERT MICHAEL WYNN

Printed in Victoria, Canada

National Library of Canada Cataloguing in Publication Data

A cataloguing record for this book that includes the U.S. Library of Congress Classification number, the Library of Congress Call number and the Dewey Decimal cataloguing code is available from the National Library of Canada. The complete cataloguing record can be obtained from the National Library's online database at: www.nlc-bnc.ca/amicus/index-e.html

ISBN 1-4120-2480-3

TRAFFORD

This book was published on-demand in cooperation with Trafford Publishing. On-demand publishing is a unique process and service of making a book available for retail sale to the public taking advantage of on-demand manufacturing and Internet marketing. On-demand publishing includes promotions, retail sales, manufacturing, order fulfilment, accounting and collecting royalties on behalf of the author.

Suite 6E, 2333 Government St., Victoria, B.C. V8T 4P4, CANADA
Phone   250-383-6864   Toll-free   1-888-232-4444 (Canada & US)
Fax   250-383-6804   E-mail   sales@trafford.com
Web site   www.trafford.com   TRAFFORD PUBLISHING IS A DIVISION OF TRAFFORD HOLDINGS LTD.
Trafford Catalogue #04-0308   www.trafford.com/robots/04-0308.html

10   9   8   7   6   5   4   3   2   1

ACKNOWLEDGEMENTS

I would like to thank the members of my family and friends who encouraged me to write my first book. I am grateful for their words of support and constructive criticism.

I would like to give special thanks to my daughter, Robin Alexia, for her valueable assistance in helping me with the finishing touches on my manuscript.

I want to thank my editor, Jennifer Jenkinsm for her professionalism and expert help in getting my book into its finished form.

Robert M. Wynn

TABLE OF CONTENTS

Preface 6

A Senseless Act of Violence 7

A Nose for Trouble 13

They called him John-John 21

The Hospital Stay .26

It's Not That Simple 35

Three Days and Counting 43

The Bus Stop Mystery 50

A View from Below
(What the devil might say about it) – Fiction 55

Interview With the Devil – Fiction 63

Wait Right Here – Fiction 68

Running Out of Time (short story) - Fiction 81

PREFACE

If you believe in God, I trust that you will find the short stories in this book enjoyable, entertaining and informative. The stories are based on my observations while wearing a law enforcement badge.

One day at the police station, a photo copier repairman shared his opinion of God's humorous side with me. The repairman said "If you want to make God laugh, go to God in prayer and tell Him about the important plans that you have made."

I would ask each reader to ponder the following questions. Select a recent day and an exact time on any day you choose. Go back exactly one year in the past to that date and time. Describe where you were and what you did. That little exercise was probably too easy for most of you. Select a date and time exactly one year in the future from the first date you chose. Now describe exactly where you will be and what you will be doing. Do you think that our heavenly Father, God Almighty could instantly and accurately answer both questions?

A Senseless Act
of Violence

Kevin, a veteran police officer, elected to attend a training class, Mental Preparation for Armed Encounters, at the Northern Virginia Criminal Justice Academy to improve his law enforcement skills. The class instructor had been teaching this class and related courses to special weapons and tactics (S.W.A.T.) law enforcement officers for a number of years. Kevin was impressed with the instructor's classroom demeanor and teaching method based on his police special operations team (S.O.T) experience. The instructor presented several videos of police related shooting incidents as training aids and one video was a portrayal of an actual shootout between a Georgia State Trooper and a motorist stopped by the trooper during a traffic detail.

Kevin was like many officers on active duty who usually fire their weapons on a regular schedule at a firing range at paper targets under controlled conditions. A survey of the seventeen officers in the class, fourteen men and three women, revealed that no one had been involved in an active police shooting. Some officers complete an entire police career without firing a single shot at a living person. The Mental Preparation course was designed to equip officers with the knowledge and skills to improve their odds of surviving an armed confrontation. The instructor survived several shootouts without injury during his police career on S.O.T. assignments.

The dynamics of a spontaneous street shootout is different than a firefighter rushing into a burning building to save the life of someone. Police officers and firefighters know the dangers and risks of their perspective occupations. Ongoing training is essential for officers and firefighters to maintain a professional readiness to serve the public at a moment's notice. Firefighters usually are protected by safety equipment before they rush into the hazardous efforts of removing people from burning structures and putting out fires. Police officers face a different challenge when they confront individuals armed with guns or edged weapons without warning at close distance and the officers' weapons are still holstered.

An individual armed with a firearm with the intent to cause bodily harm will cause a certain amount of fear and panic in most people regardless of their professional training or status. A person with an exposed gun can aim and fire in two seconds or less. Many police departments train officers to respond to simulated armed encounters by engaging quick flipping paper targets with pictures of men and women holding various weapons.

The ideal response to the unexpected sight of a firearm at close range is to seek the nearest protective cover, draw your weapon and defend yourself. The response drills are intended to cause the officer to instinctively react in a manner that will afford the officer the chance to defend his life in a disadvantageous circumstance. Most of the shooting incidents occur at close range and are over in a matter of a few seconds. Officers are encouraged to constantly practice a quick draw technique and practice dry firing an unloaded weapon to become the best shooter possible. A second place finish in a shootout with one or more individuals is not the preferred position for any police officer.

Kevin had seen the highlighted TV news coverage of the video of Trooper Mark Coates' shooting incident on a couple of occasions prior to viewing it again in the Mental Preparation class. Kevin did not realize how actual much horror was associated with the shooting incident because a lot of video footage had been edited for viewing on TV. At the beginning of the classroom video Trooper Coates displayed the appearance of a highly disciplined officer in excellent physical shape conducting a traffic stop. The former Marine wore his state trooper uniform with obvious pride.

Trooper Coates had an air of confidence and seemed to be in control of the situation while talking to the motorist. The driver was standing outside of his vehicle with both of his hands in his pant pockets. Trooper Coates explained the nature of his drug enforcement detail and was asking for permission to search the trunk of the motorist's vehicle for illegal drugs or alcohol when the motorist removed one hand from his right pant pocket, pointed a small gun at the trooper and issued a death threat. Each of the students in the class seemed to experience the same sense of shock when the motorist removed his hand from his pant pocket holding a firearm.

The class watched the video in stunned silence as Trooper Coates tried to persuade the motorist to lower the gun as Trooper Coates attempted to back away with his arms raised. The motorist began firing point blank at the officer. The wounded officer managed to draw his weapon and fire at the motorist before he collapsed on the ground. The motorist jumped into his vehicle and fled the scene. The motorist was apprehended by other members of the Georgia State Police, prosecuted in court and sentenced to prison for the shooting death of Trooper Coates.

On each of the subsequent occasions while watching other videos, Kevin found himself feeling the same intensity of heart-ache. The pain and stress was always there when he saw the actual footage of a brother officer killed in the line of duty. Kevin noticed that he could visualize himself in the role of the officers portrayed in the various scenes because he was still on active police duty. He was reminded of the warning taught in his first traffic enforcement class in the police academy. There is no such thing as a routine traffic stop until the officer has returned safely to his cruiser and the motorist has driven away with a traffic citation or a warning.

Kevin watched the videos in the classroom to detect possible tactical errors and to improve training techniques for law enforcement officers. He made a startling realization and concluded that the same concept would apply to any living person.

If one were to freeze frame a critical moment of anyone's mortal life, one would notice that all living individuals are subject to being caught in a very stressful life threatening predicament. At any given moment in our lifetime, all of us are "Caught between Coming and Going." We had no say in when, where or how we were born. Most of us will have no say in when, where or how we leave this earth.

It had been the personal opinion of Kevin that in situations when one person has control over another person's life by whatever means, it is a moral test for the person seemingly in control. To unjustifiably take a person's life is morally corrupt and violates God's Commandment, Thou shall not kill. Most people view the helpless individual as a victim rather than seeing that individual as someone with a role in the battle of good versus evil.

The videotape of Trooper Coates' death gave law enforcement officers, the rare opportunity to analyze an actual shoot out. Officers on a similar journey in life can empathize with Trooper Coates' experience in that circumstance at the end of his mortal life. The video made it possible to witness a good man caught at a moment between his coming into this world and leaving it. Each person with a date of birth should have a realistic expectation about their date of departure from this earth at an unknown date and time in the future. Our mortal journey on this earth is a temporary one.

Prior to showing some of the videos of actual shooting events and some re-enacted scenarios, Kevin noticed the sense of relief the instructor got when he mentioned that certain officers shown in the videos had recovered from their injuries and returned to active law enforcement duty. Sharing that personal information took the edge off some of the stress that Kevin felt while watching the officers injured on screen.

It was an additional comfort for Kevin to remember that the final results of all events are within God's Will. Pain is a part of the process of living. Recognizing and understanding pain is to realize that all is not well. Something needs to be fixed or healed.

The instructor knew Trooper Coates personally and shared with Kevin that he was a good family man in addition to being a good law enforcement officer. Trooper Coates was a Christian and had accepted Christ Jesus as his personal Savior many years prior to the senseless act of violence recorded on the video camera in his state police car on the night of his death.

A Nose
For Trouble

Kevin, the veteran police officer, was drinking a cup of coffee with his old friend, Nathan. They worked the evening patrol shifts together on many occasions. When the street activities were slow on Kevin's beat, the K-9 officer and Kevin took turns buying the coffee and met at their favorite hang-out spot. Nathan loved to talk. He knew something about everything. Nathan found Kevin to be a good listener.

Nathan told Kevin about his latest problems regarding Max, his canine partner. Kevin thought to himself how often in police work, some of the actual cases seemed stranger than fiction. Nathan graduated from the police academy in the class session ahead of Kevin. Nathan joined the force with the intention of being a K-9 handler as soon as possible. Nathan got his lucky break when one of the K-9 officers was promoted to patrol sergeant and created a vacancy on the K-9 squad. Nathan reported for K-9 training at the time Sergeant Stump, the training coordinator, made up his mind to get rid of Max.

Max was the biggest German Shepherd in his litter of four. Shortly after his birth, Max was forecasted to be an exceptionally big dog. The predictions came true. Max was the largest German Shepherd Sgt. Stump had ever trained. It didn't take long for the other K-9 officers to notice that Max was super aggressive. During the training drills, Max would work his way up and down the training sleeve trying to bite the person wearing the sleeve acting as the bad guy. Max exhibited more enthusiasm in the biting drills than any other dog in Sgt. Stump's recent memory.

Nathan was 6'4", 285 lbs. and he improved on his college football conditioning since joining the police department. Nathan fell for Max the moment he saw the big German Shepherd in the kennel on his first day. Sgt. Stump observed Nathan's reaction to Max and wondered if he was the handler for Max. Nathan had the size to take on the challenge. Nathan convinced Sgt. Stump to let Max train as Nathan's partner in the K-9 officer and dog obedience academy. They finished the session as the top handler and dog team.

Sgt. Stump transferred the heat he received from the police chief to Nathan. Nathan had to write almost as many dog bite and property damage reports as Sgt. Stump regarding Max's building searches. Max had turned into a K-9 Jeckyll and Hyde. When Max was off duty with Nathan, Max was gentle around children of all ages. He displayed a passive indifference around females. Most females were content to admire Max's K-9 looks and size from a distance. On duty Max was a burglar's worst terror. If a burglar was in the building when Max went in, it wasn't a question of whether Max would find the burglar or not. The question was how soon could Nathan get Max off the suspect to cut down on the medical bill.

If a burglar had struck and left the building before Nathan and Max conducted a building search, Nathan would have to write a property damage report more often than not. Max would chew on door knobs, the legs of furniture or anything chewable if there was no suspect inside to bite. Nathan had to give Max the freedom to do an effective building search. It was a challenge for Nathan to get to Max and put him on a leash before Max started his chewing routine.

City Hall was in an uproar over Max's last dog bite. The political heat under the police chief was intense. The police chief was rumored to have said, "Thank God, the suspect wasn't a juvenile." The case involved a good silent burglar alarm received at the police communications center. Two patrol officers arrived on the scene and set up a good perimeter watch on the business before Nathan and Max arrived. Nathan issued the proper police challenge for the suspect to give up before he sent Max in to check the building. The suspect was hiding in an office closet on the third floor.

Max picked up the suspect's scent while he was working the first floor. Nathan noticed Max became more excited as he continued searching on the second floor. Max went on full alert when they reached the third floor. Nathan knew that Max knew that somebody was going to get bit and pretty soon. As Max entered the office where the suspect was hiding in the closet, Max sounded like a wounded bear fighting for his life. Max slammed against the closet door and started chewing on the door knob. The suspect urinated in his clothes and began crying. He yelled to Nathan, "Okay I give up, get your dog. I give up."

Nathan gave Max the "on guard" command and pointed for him to stay at a spot in front of the closet door. Nathan opened the door and ordered the suspect to come out with his hands up. The suspect was crying as he inched toward the open door with his hands raised. Max glared at the suspect as the hair on his back bristled and a rumbling low growl started rising from Max's throat.

Nathan wanted to get handcuffs on the suspect as soon as possible and check him for weapons. Nathan also wanted to verify that the man was alone in the building. Nathan had another concern. He wanted to get Max on a lead sooner rather than later. The suspect took another step toward the open door with his hand raised and without warning fell backward. Nathan heard himself yelling, "Max, stay. Max, stay." It seemed that Nathan's words and his actions were in slow motion. When the suspect moved backward, Max dashed toward the open door like a bolt of lightning. The patrol officers outside winced at the sound of the burglar's high pitched scream. One of the officers called for an ambulance and the patrol watch commander. He was well aware of Max's reputation.

Nathan told Kevin that this might be Max's last week on active duty. The suspect's attorney had already filed an excessive force lawsuit while police Internal Affairs investigation was just getting started. At that moment, Nathan and Kevin were given a radio dispatch to meet Vice Detective Floyd at an apartment in the high rent district of their city.

Vice Detective Floyd had done his homework very well on this case and he was not going to leave anything to chance on this investigation. Floyd obtained a valid search warrant for Iceberg Slim's apartment from a circuit court judge earlier that afternoon. Floyd assigned four narcotics detectives from his unit, two homicide detectives with prior vice experience and six members of the Special Operations Team (S.O.T) the task of entering the apartment. Floyd chose four of the most experienced patrol officers working on the evening shift to assist on staffing the perimeter around the apartment building. Floyd knew Kevin's record of successful catches during foot pursuits. Kevin had eight catches and no escapes. During a foot chase, if Kevin saw you, he would catch you.

Iceberg Slim was a heavy hitter in the drug business. He had operated with success for several years in the city. Slim had done well by staying off the radar screens of the local vice units. It was Floyd's lucky day that Iceberg Slim's name came up during the investigation of a big deal scheduled to go down in Floyd's town.

Peabody, Donald White, was released from the adult detention center exactly one week ago, Saturday. He was determined to make the best of this opportunity to get a cut of some big action going down at Iceberg Slim's apartment. Peabody knew that he was entering into a risky deal. Two days ago, Peabody's probation officer, Henry Tucker, told Peabody that he would have to serve the remaining three years of his drug conviction sentence if Peabody got anything more than a traffic ticket at anytime during his probationary period. Peabody owed his inside connection in the detention center a favor for setting Peabody up with this meeting with Iceberg Slim. Peabody's hands were sweaty slightly as the cab got closer to upscale apartments in wealthier section of the city. He was about to cross the point of no return.

Peabody prided himself on playing outside of society's rules. He wanted to take the easy way or short cut rather than putting forth the effort to make an honest living. The warning from his probation officer was like water running off a duck's back. Peabody knew that he was to cool to get caught by the police anytime soon. He was hooking up with big time professionals in the drug business. Peabody entered the apartment building without attracting any attention. He was admitted into Slim's apartment when Peabody gave the code "Let's do it."

Kevin was positioned on the corner of the apartment building. Floyd told him to watch the bedroom window carefully when the entry went in. The window was six feet above the ground. The balcony at the kitchen would be the most probable route for an escape attempt. The balcony was covered by a S.O.T. officer. Floyd was not leaving any to chance on this operation. Floyd told Nathan to let Max do his thing if anyone got past the perimeter around the outside of the apartment. Nathan said, "This may be our last party and Max's last chance dance. If someone comes our way, Max will get him. You can bank on it." Floyd knocked on the apartment. Someone looked through the peephole. Floyd knocked on the door again, announced "Police officers. Open the door." The entry team had to use the battering ram to pop the door. Immediately there was a lot of scurrying inside the apartment by the occupants as the entry team began grabbing people and collecting evidence.

It was a chilly night outside. Kevin noticed that frost had formed on the grass behind the apartment building. When the entry team popped the front door, Kevin heard the commotion inside. He stepped back and looked up at the bedroom window. The window blinds were closed. A light was on in the bedroom. Kevin heard the crinkling of the blinds at about the same time the glass pane shattered. Pieces of glass rained down. Kevin shielded his eyes with his right hand and instinctively drew his service weapon as a body came torpedoing through the blinds. The man landed on the broken glass face down with his arms stretched out. Within two seconds after hitting the ground the man began thrashing around in obvious pain. Kevin shouted at the man, "Police, don't move." He kept his service revolver aimed at the suspect. The S.O.T. officer ran over and placed handcuffs on the man. The suspect began yelling, "I need a doctor, I'm cut." Kevin and the S.O.T. officer picked the man up as Detective Floyd came running around the corner.

Detective Floyd looked at the man and asked, "Peabody what are you doing here? Does your probation officer know that you are hanging out with drug dealers? What happened to your nose?" Detective Floyd called for the medic unit at the staging area. The medics responded to treat the deep gash on Peabody's nose and the cuts on his hands. No one escaped from the apartment.

Kevin thanked God that night for another blessed day at work. It was a good day for the law enforcement team. Kevin wondered if Floyd had prayed to God for the success of his mission. Detective Floyd had worked on this drug investigation for many months. Floyd's careful planning and attention to the smallest details paid off with the successful arrest of some big drug deal-ers Iceberg Slim had been operating on the dark side for so long, Kevin wondered if Slim even knew how to pray. Kevin doubted that Peabody had prayed to God for success in his plan to get some quick easy money from a drug deal. Kevin chuckled at the thought that God would be amused when some people begin their prayer with "God I have made these plans."

Peabody' parole officer charged him with associating with a known criminal, a violation of the rules of his probation. He was sent back to prison for three years.

Iceberg Slim, identified as Claude Haney, was charged with possession of cocaine with the intent to distribute a controlled drug. Slim's attorney bailed him out of jail after his first court appearance.

Max broke his right front leg when he jumped from a second floor balcony chasing a burglary suspect. Max was retired from police duty.

THEY CALLED
HIM JOHN-JOHN

John-John knew that he was in trouble when the pain in his chest kept him from sleeping for a second straight night. He had noticed the gradual fading of his strength and a nagging tiredness that he could not shake. John-John was no longer able to play basketball with his regular crew because he could not run up and down the court with the slowest player on the team. He had not gone swimming in over a month. John-John loved to swim, something was terribly wrong. Reluctantly John-John knew that he could not postpone going to the doctor any longer.

John-John thought about the many times he had stood around the smoke break areas, puffing on a cigarette. He enjoyed the company and the conversations of the other smokers. It pained him to think of the warnings from his good friend Kevin, a veteran police officer. Over the years Kevin told John-John to seriously consider giving up smoking. John-John told Kevin that smoking was his only real vice. He smoked because he really enjoyed the taste and relaxation of a good cigarette.

The physical exam, the follow-up tests and the doctor's findings knocked the bottom out of John-John's day. There were cancerous spots on both of his lungs. The cancer had snuck up and pounced on John-John like a 800 pound grizzly bear. The knock down blow was delivered when the doctor told John-John that he wasn't able to return to street duty.

John-John entered the police service on March 24, 1982. During his 18 years of police service, he worked with most of the officers and employees at the police department at one time or another. John-John was the friend who patiently listened to what you had to say. He was willing to share some of his personal experiences in the conversation.

Some of their conversations were heart to heart talks that caused Kevin to think about the topics and John-John long after they parted company. It was not uncommon for Kevin to think about John-John from time to time and wonder how he was doing in his illness. Kevin wondered about John-John one morning. He remembered a conversation they had about their daughters. John-John believed that some people didn't think to talk to God about Jesus when they talked to God during their quiet time. John-John enlightened Kevin to the fact that God is like many parents who enjoy talking about their children. A person may be a total stranger to you but they will share intimate details about their children during a conversation. John-John told Kevin that he talked to God regularly during his quiet time.

A good friend is priceless. John-John and Kevin frequently talked about their Savior, Jesus Christ, on various occasions. When Kevin thought about John-John that morning, he found himself thinking about John-John's other Friend. The thought of Jesus gave Kevin the relief of knowing that John-John was alright. If Kevin had to choose just one friend to have, his decision would be very easy. Without a moment's hesitation his choice would be the name above all other names in the book of life, Christ Jesus.

There are some questions on the minds of people at some home going gatherings that the wisest of men can't answer.

- Why is the length of people's lives different?
- How long will this pain (the heartache of losing a loved one) last?
- How far am I into my twenty-four hour day?
- What was he (or she) thinking about at the moment before his/her physical death?
- Can I get a passing mark for my race even though I have spent most of my time sitting on the bench or standing on the sideline of life?

The response the wise men wisely give to the above questions is only God knows.

Kevin thought about the impact that significant people had made on his life. He thought deeply about the message or purpose of different individual's lives and how it related to Kevin's purpose on earth. Whenever Kevin thought of John-John, he noticed that he smiled. Kevin could picture John-John's smile and remembered John-John's comment about the "faith of a mustard seed." John-John believed that as one's knowledge about religion increased, one's faith in God increased. He asked Kevin to ponder the number of times a day that people called out God's name and their reason for calling to Him. Can you begin to imagine the number of times that some people call on God for selfish reasons. John-

John wondered if the petty call were a distraction to God from the really important daily matters in the world? Especially when you compare it to the number of people calling on God in a day for things they want rather than things they really need.

John-John stated with certainty while he was under the doctor's care that he was going to beat his cancer diagnosis. He was happy about his method of praying to God for specific results. John-John prayed for the right doctor, the right medicine and that the medicine would be effective. John-John was on an emotional high after completing his radiation treatments when one of his examinations revealed no signs of the cancer in his body. He recovered his strength and returned to active police duty.

John-John had several periodic cancer free examinations. His swimming ability developed to the point where he could complete eighty laps during a regular workout. Kevin told John-John that his testimonial was a sparkling example of the power of prayer and a message of inspiration for other people.

During Kevin's last significant conversation with John-John, he told Kevin, "He was not going to let the devil steal his joy." Kevin did not know at the time that John-John's cancer had returned. John-John had attended a religious service and the text of the message pertained to God's gifts for us. The minister talked about circumstances that cause people to miss out on gifts from God because they are not focused on God at the right time in their life. The minister threw out several small rubber balls of different colors amongst the audience to illustrate his point.

John-John sat on the far left end in the front row of seats in the church. The balls were thrown from the front podium in an arc over John-John's head. The people in the audience who managed to catch one of the rubber balls had to focus on where the ball were being thrown and scramble out of their seat to get one. As the rubber balls were tossed out John-John found himself wanting to have one of the balls.

The speaker threw the last ball in a high arc over John-John's head toward the rear of the church. John-John said that he turned and watched the ball bounce off a rear ceiling beam, ricochet off a sidewall, bounce into the aisle and head in his direction. John-John jumped out of his seat and caught the ball in the air.

When Kevin reflects on John-John's testimony regarding his colored ball of joy Kevin is reminded of a song, "My precious gift" from the Master. A gift that is more precious than all the diamonds, silver and gold. The gift of life, when God gave me my soul.

John-John worked six months on the streets as a patrol officer before his cancer caused him to go on light duty. His illness zapped his strength quickly. John-John returned to the hospital for medical treatment. He did not stay in the hospital long.

John-John was a long time friend of Kevin's. He completed his mortal journey on this earth on September 6, 2000.

Kevin has been running for the Lord for some time. He has matured and gained much wisdom along the way. Kevin had the pleasure of running with his good friend John-John for awhile. Kevin's goal is to run to the last step of the last mile of his journey on earth. Kevin has been running to hear the Master say, "A job well done my son, welcome home." Kevin feels confident that John-John earned the privilege to hear those treasured words from his Heavenly Father.

THE HOSPITAL STAY

Jack and Helen were proud of their son, James, from the moment of his birth. They realized how special James was early in his mid infancy months. James would rarely wake up during the night. Helen noticed that her son was cheerful most of the time. James started walking when he was nine months old. James had his moments in his first year of life but compared to the majority of normal babies, Helen and Jack had it made.

Helen worked from her home part time on her computer. She worked on a select group of financial accounts for a major insurance company. Helen's job provided her with a lavish salary and many home hours to spend with her young son. Helen devoted a lot of time toward James' education.

Jack and Helen were constantly amazed at how quickly James absorbed information. During his third year of life both of James' parents were convinced that James had the mental talents of a genius. James mind was like an encyclopedia. It was obvious that James had a photographic memory. He could remember conversations and data after hearing it one time. James could recall the information years later and repeat verbatim exactly what had been said to the last period.

James began to lose his sight at the age of five. His parents took James to the best optometrist for treatment. James was diagnosed as having eyeritis, an uncommon disease that was causing his irises to malfunction. A second and third opinion by equally qualified optometrists confirmed the eye disease as eyeritis. James had contracted a very aggressive form of the disease. Jack and Helen took James back to the first doctor, Dr. Hilton.

Dr. Hilton had treated a few cases of eyeritis with a combination of medicines and the results were successful. There was no known cause of eyeritis and no one had discovered a cure for the disease. Dr. Hilton's prescriptions only helped James for a short time. James was completely blind on his sixth birthday.

James was loved dearly by the numerous members on both sides of his family. Each of James' classmates remembered him as the courageous blind boy that was a straight "A" student in all of his classes. They admired James' quick wit when he made them laugh. The maturity of his knowledge and the extent of his intelligence fascinated the other students when James talked to them. Occasionally James' friends felt sorry that James could not participate in some of the action games of soccer, basketball, baseball and volleyball. James accepted his limitations in those areas and James' friends found him to be an inspiring cheer person on the sidelines.

James loved to attend Bible school and the regular church service with his parents on Sunday. Ms. Cotton was James' Bible study leader at their church. James was her favorite and she felt that James was destined to be a great man in the religious field. Pastor Smith enjoyed the times when he heard James talking to the students in Bible study. James was responding to the question, "Why do you love the Lord?"

James gave the following response: "I love the Lord, my God because God loved me first. God gave me life, my soul and his precious Son, Jesus Christ. I love God with all my heart because he gave me my family, friends and all of the blessings in my life. I love God because He is all Good, all the time. I love God because He promised me that He would be with me always and forever."

James had just turned seventeen when he received a letter from Dr. Hilton. Jack and Helen were excited when they read his comments. Dr. Hilton had been following the latest developments in laser eye surgery. He was impressed with the laboratory achievements by an exceptionally skilled eye surgeon, Dr. Taylor.

Dr. Taylor made an early reputation of stardom in the surgery field because of his successful laser surgery that restored the sight in four blind patients. Dr. Hilton wanted James' parents to consider James for laser eye surgery. Dr. Taylor agreed with Dr. Hilton's recommendation because James was able to see during the early years of his youth.

Dr. Taylor was anxious to meet James. Dr. Hilton had talked Dr. Taylor's ear off about the exceptional intelligence of his young patient. Dr. Taylor graduated with the third highest grade point average in the history of his medical university. Dr. Taylor was confident that he could hold his ground with young master James.

James found Dr. Taylor to be very charming and James' parents thought him to be rather young looking for an accomplished laser eye surgeon. Dr. Taylor's examination of James' eyes revealed that James would be a good candidate for the laser surgery. Dr. Taylor told James and his parents that he could not guarantee the restoration of James' eye sight, but Dr. Taylor liked the odds very much. Jack, Helen and James were thrilled by Dr. Taylor's assessment of James' opportunity to see again. They agreed to schedule a date for the operation.

As the family prepared to leave, Dr. Taylor said, "Not so fast. I have a couple of questions to ask this young man."

James was startled for a brief moment but he responded, "Really."

Dr. Taylor came back with "Yes, really."

Dr. Taylor asked James to define light.

James answered, "Light is part of the electromagnetic spectrum that includes infrared radiation, radio waves, gamma rays, X-rays and ultraviolet radiation. The human eye can detect and interpret the visible light band of the electromagnetic spectrum."

Dr. Taylor smiled at James and said, "Not bad. Not bad at all.

Do you know how fast light travels?"

Jack and Helen looked at each other.

James said, "According to Einstein's theory of Relativity light travels at a constant speed of 299, 792, 458 meters per second. Stated another way, one mile equals 1, 760 yards, 176 footballs lined up in a row equals one mile. Light can travel 170,337 miles in a second."

Dr. Taylor said, "That's right. What is time?"

James said, "According to Isaac Newton, absolute, true and mathematical time, also known as duration is the measurement of motion. The increments of time are seconds, minutes, hours, days, weeks, months and years."

Dr. Taylor shook James' hand and said " James, you are the man. I will see you on surgery day."

James gave Dr. Taylor a hug and said, "Dr. Taylor, I like you too."

Jack and Helen checked James into the hospital Thursday evening for the scheduled laser surgery on Friday morning at 8:00 a.m. James had to complete some preliminary medical procedures so that he would be ready for surgery in the morning. James' parents stayed with him until the evening visiting hours were over. Jack and Helen told their son that they would see him bright and early in the morning.

Friday morning before the surgery, James was displaying symptoms of a respiratory infection. The hospital staff doctor, Dr. Springs and Dr. Taylor agreed that James' surgery should be postponed and set for another day. Dr. Springs told Jack and Helen that he wanted to keep James in the hospital under observation for the rest of the day. The doctor was concerned about the rapid growth rate of the infection on James' respiratory system.

Jack and Helen received a phone call Friday afternoon to come to the hospital right away. James had been moved to an isolated room in the intensive care unit. Jack and Helen could only visit with James for a short time in the I.C.U. room. They spent most of the evening in the cafeteria and some time in the visitor's waiting room. When the evening visiting hours were over, Dr. Springs authorized Jack and Helen to spend some extra precious time with their son. Helen had given birth to James in that same hospital.

James felt the heavy weight on his parent's shoulders during Jack and Helen's visit. James thought about the numerous mornings of early quiet time with God. James suddenly became aware of the calmness that came over his body. He could not see this new visitor but James knew that a messenger was standing next to his bed.

My name is Joshua. "I have been sent here to ask you some questions. You may find these questions a bit more challenging than Dr. Taylor's little warm up drill."

The smile that James felt inside beamed on his face.

Joshua. "Which hero in the Bible did you find to be the most interesting after your favorite hero?"

James wanted some of this action.

James asked his own questions. "Well Joshua, who was my favorite hero?"

Joshua knew the question before James had asked it. "Our favorite hero is the same as yours and the one whom God chose as His favorite, Jesus."

James began to explain why Paul was his second favorite hero of the bible. "The transition Saul made during his period of blindness to become Paul, the very capable spokesman of Christianity."

Joshua asked James, "Have you noticed the pattern of questions some people ask when someone has been involved in a car accident?"

"Yes, Joshua, I have. People usually want to know was he or she injured? Will he or she be alright? How much damage was done to the vehicles? Who was at fault? Did they have car insurance? What is the name of the insurance company?"

"James, you know that God gives his children "free will" as a gift. With "free will" comes responsibility. Some of them can't wait for the opportunity and the experience of driving a car. Some of them set out on the short journey of driving a car without the proper skills, they don't want to use the seat belts, some don't have a driver's license and too many of them drive without the required car insurance."

Joshua. "When did your heavenly Father decide that you would spend time on this earth? When did he determine the date of your birth and how long you would stay here? Who knew exactly where you would be born on the date that your mother became pregnant with you?"

James said, "Joshua, I am my Heavenly Father's humble servant. I love God with all of my heart. His choice of parents for me was excellent. I had tried to be mindful to thank God for the many blessings that He has bestowed on me. I have always appreciated the love given to me by my family and friends. I am forever thankful to God for my soul and my Saviour, Christ Jesus and my life. Joshua, only God knows the answers to the questions that you just asked."

Joshua. "James, it is important that you know that God had planned for your return to Him before he sent you to earth. Your stay on earth like the rest of his children is only temporary. God assigns each one a time frame according to His will.

With "free will" comes the responsibility to get the life insurance policy that will cover your soul when the mortal journey ends.

James when you chose Christ Jesus as your Saviour, you made the right decision. When you chose Jesus, you chose ever-lasting life. Jesus is the only insurance for the soul that can guarantee your assurance of entry into Heaven.

Don't be sad for the faithful ones that you are leaving behind. God knows the extent and their purpose during their stay on earth.

Your heavenly Father knows everything that they will endure according to his Will. Always remember that everything above and beneath the Heavens belong to Almighty God.

God will always care and look out for his faithful. Remember the following: Moses, the parting of the Red Sea; Noah, the Ark for the great flood; the deliverance of Shadrach, Meshach and Abed-Nego from the fiery furnace of Nebuchadmezzar and Daniel from Darius' lions den."

Joshua. "James, I want you to blink your eyes, it is time to go."

James blinked his eyes and looked at Joshua.

James could not ever remember seeing an angel before. Joshua was a most beautiful sight for James to see.

The only thing James could say was "Oh my God." He said it twice, "Oh my God." Joshua had heard that exact expression and the joy it contained on countless occasions. It always sounded to him as good the last time as it did the first time Joshua heard it. "Oh my God" what a wonderful expression. Such a beautiful sound.

By the time Jack and Helen arrived at their home. James had gone with Joshua to wait for them with his Heavenly Father.

It's Not
That Simple

Here today, gone tomorrow. They were in the wrong place at the wrong time. It is as simple as that. The ignorant man planted his feet firmly on his soapbox, stuck out his chest and proudly said, "It is just that simple. My mind is made up; so don't try to confuse me with the facts."

Understanding the difference between life on earth and mortal death and the timing of an individual's death requires knowledge of God's Plan. The concept of eternity and eternal life is not easily understood by the untrained average mind. The following scientific experiment is offered as evidence of the above position. Six large metal bins of the same weight and dimensions were placed on separate scales. A half ton of aluminum was placed in the 1st bin, a half ton of glass in the 2nd bin, a half ton of crushed mountain rocks in the 3rd bin, a half ton of iron in the 4th bin and a haft ton of cotton in the 5th bin. A 1,000 pounds of hardened steel was place in the 6th bin. Which of the six bins registered the heaviest weight on the scales?

If your answer was the hardened steel, that answer was incorrect. If you chose the crushed mountain rocks, that answer was incorrect. If you chose either aluminum, cotton, glass or iron, that answer was incorrect. The correct answer for the scientific experiment was that each scale registered the same weight. Those individuals with the learned knowledge that a half ton equals a 1,000 pounds stood the best chance of understanding the question and reciting the correct answer. How long is a lifetime minus the time spent on earth?

So it is with the concept of the line between life and death. In some cases the time span is less than tomorrow. Here today, gone today. The line between life and death can range from a scant second to a few hours. Such was the case in the lives of two men, Antwon and Perry, known to Officer Kevin. Antwon Dixon and Perry Evans came from different backgrounds. Both of them made it past the age of 21 without unordinary difficulty. Neither of the two young men lived to experience their twenty-ninth birthday.

Kevin was in the last stage of his grieving over the accidental death of Antwon Dixon, a fellow police officer killed in a motorcycle accident, when he learned about the senseless death of his second cousin, Perry Evans. Kevin felt the sting in his eyes as the burning tears began to trickle slowly down his face.

The echo in Kevin's mind kept repeating, "Here I go again", as the pain in his heart throbbed with each heartbeat. This latest news over the telephone regarding the death of his cousin, Perry, caused his mind to flash back to the previous Wednesday morning. Kevin rolled over and turned the radio alarm off at 6:00 A.M. He decided to get an extra ten minutes snooze before getting dressed for work. Kevin hoped that his decision would not cause him to be late for the 7:30 A.M. roll call.

As luck would have it, the unusually heavy traffic pattern caused Kevin to feel the stress of being late for roll call. Kevin got to a parking space on the employee's parking lot with only minutes to go before the start of roll call. Kevin dreaded the thought of walking into the roll call room as the roll call sergeant gave the daily assignments and the momentary silence that followed the tardy person to the closest empty seat. Kevin saw the police cruiser parked on the curb in front of the police station as he rushed down the sidewalk toward the front door. The black draping across the cruiser and the black banner over the front door signaled that an officer had died.

Kevin had not heard of any news reports of an officer killed in the line of duty over the last two days; so he reasoned that a retired police officer had been called home.

Kevin sat down in a chair exactly at 7:30 A.M. as the roll call began. There was a heavy presence of sadness in the room. Duke, a junior police officer spoke first. Duke said that he would brief the roll call because he was on the scene at the time of accident. Kevin heard Duke say that Antwon had died in surgery on Monday afternoon from injuries Antwon received during a motorcycle accident that morning.

The pain struck Kevin like a load of bricks. The pain was immediate, sharp and cruel. Kevin had just seen Antwon Dixon Sunday, three days before the end of their two day break. He recalled the smile on Antwon's handsome face and the familiar friendly sound of the greeting in Antwon's voice. Kevin's friend had been called home suddenly and unexpectedly.

Duke said that the four friends; Antwon, Tony, Bellefonte and he, were riding on that pleasant Monday morning on the open highway. Duke described the riding conditions as perfect for that time of the morning. Kevin fondly remembered his motorcycle riding days and the thrill of a long highway ride with seven other motorcyclists. It seemed almost impossible to describe the sense of freedom and exhilaration one feels on a motorcycle on the open road to someone who has never operated or ridden on a motorcycle.

Antwon, Tony and Duke noticed that Bellefonte had fallen behind. In the process of slowing down to turn around, Antwon appeared to have gripped his front brake too hard. The front end of his bike dipped down suddenly which caused Antwon to be thrown off the motorcycle over the handlebars. Antwon landed on the highway in front of his motorcycle. To the astonishment of Duke and Tony, Antwon's motorcycle bounced into the air and landed on top of Antwon. Duke used his cell phone to call an ambulance. Antwon was conscious and asked about his girlfriend as he was being taken to the hospital in the ambulance. Antwon died that Monday afternoon in surgery.

Antwon was 28 years old at the time of his death. He was a good officer and well liked by everyone that worked with him. Kevin had worked several cases with Antwon. Kevin would miss the young officer. Kevin felt saddened by the news of his cousin's death, but he was surprised that Perry's death caused him a less painful heartache initially than the report of Antwon's death. Kevin had not seen Perry in six years. He had to search his memory to recall the smiling face of his cousin.

Perry went to a local hamburger restaurant with a male friend. Kevin's mother said that her great-nephew and the other young man were sitting in a car on the parking lot talking to three young ladies. A jealous male acquaintance of one of the young ladies told Perry and the other young man to stop talking to them. Perry was exchanging telephone numbers with one of the women when the jealous acquaintance fired a handgun at the car. Several shots were fired before the gunman jumped into a car and rode away with his friends.

Perry was struck one time under his arm. The bullet entered his heart and killed him instantly. He was 24 years old. The other young man in the car with Perry was hit three times on various parts of his body. He was taken to the hospital by ambulance for medical treatment. The doctor predicted that he would recover from his wounds. Kevin reasoned that the shooting of his cousin was another senseless act of violence.

After investigating numerous cases of homicides, sudden deaths from vehicle accidents, and sucides, Kevin has seen the face of death on many individuals over the course of his police career. Each case was different with its specific set of circumstances. Some people wondered if some deaths were the result of individuals being in the wrong place at the wrong time. There are records of airplane crashes with no survivors. Some planes filled with people have crashed and there have been one or two survivors. The others on the plane perished. Kevin concluded that God has the last word. When the Master calls for someone, it doesn't matter where they are, what they are doing or the time of day, the mortal body will cease to live.

Watching the lives of people from behind the badge of a sworn law enforcement officer is a special priviledge. The public's trust in the integrity of police officers is the foundation that supports the authority given to officers to enforce the laws made by the elected officials. The badge of authority does not make police officers immune from feeling the grief that everyday people feel on some occasions.

Officer Kevin was on patrol one afternoon when he observed a driver run a red light. The light had been red for four seconds. The driver did not attempt to slow down. Officer Kevin stopped the car.

Officer Kevin. "May I see your driver's license and registration card?"

Driver. The driver gave Officer Kevin his license and registration card without saying a word.

Officer Kevin. "Sir, I stopped you for running the red light. I am going to cite you for the traffic violation."

Driver. "OK." The response was made in a subdued manner. The driver stared ahead.

Officer Kevin paused before walking to his cruiser and asked, "Sir, why didn't you stop for the red light?"

Driver. "I did not intend to disobey the law. I just found out that my mother died this morning. I was driving around to get some fresh air."

Officer Kevin. "Sir, I am sorry for your loss. I offer you my deepest condolences. Driving around in your condition is not a good idea. You could have killed someone by driving through the intersection against a red light. Do you have a minister or a close relative to talk to?"

Driver. "I do but I would like to get a cup of coffee first."

Officer Kevin. "There is a McDonalds up ahead. I will follow there. I will let you go with a warning for the red light infraction. I know this is a bad time for you right now. Anytime you are driving a motor vehicle, you have a responsibility to other drivers on the highway."

A frequent saying "Thank God for Jesus" by one of Kevin's aunts has been a valued reference point for Kevin in his comprehension of the unexpected difficulties encountered in everyday life. Kevin has appreciated the awesome power of the Lord's Prayer as a moral compass and a solid foundation for understanding those circumstances that can overwhelm a person's emotions unexpectedly. Kevin has also known the value of the 23rd Psalm during times of physical stress and discomfort. He viewed the 23rd Psalm as a beacon of light that can cut through the darkness of difficult times.

Kevin thought back on some news reporters' descriptions of killer thunderstorms, hurricanes, floods, earthquakes and tornadoes. The news anchors reported the widespread property damage and the number of people who lost their lives during the disasters. Often times the number of lives lost when compared to the amount of property damage and the repair estimates was very small. Some people are inclined to say, "They were at the wrong place at the wrong time." Kevin reflected on the Lord's Prayer and thought to himself, when it involves a matter of life or death, the answer is in the prayer. Jesus gave us the Lord's Prayer as an example of proper prayer and a key to a better understanding of God. He stated it best in the verse referring to God, "Thy will be done in earth as it is in Heaven." Kevin regarded the Lord's prayer as his sun and the 23rd Psalm as his moon to light up his dark times.

THREE DAYS
AND COUNTING

Jenny felt extremely tired from running errands that began right after her sunrise breakfast on her back deck on September 10, 2001. It wasn't often that she took the time to cook breakfast at home and enjoy the beautiful view of her back yard that stopped at the tree line of Forest Haven Estates. Jenny was a doer. Her "to do" list never seemed to end. She laughed to herself quietly because she was constantly adding tasks to her list of things to do for her friends. Yesterday, Beth, her best friend was confined to bed rest for three days because of a strained back.

Jenny felt compelled to complete Beth's portion of the assignment to get cards and fruit baskets for sick and shut in members of their church. It was ironic that Beth would receive a card and a fruit basket because Jenny was that kind of a friend. Jenny felt overwhelmed for a brief few moments. It seemed that she was carrying the weight of the world on her shoulders. Some of the committee chairpersons in her church seemed to miss the spirit of the Pastor Lane's recommendation concerning volunteers. Pastor Lane suggested that busy people were the best candidates to select for soliciting assistance to complete church tasks. People with time on their hand tended to be procrastinators. Procrastinators are prone to giving excuses for not completing a task that was due yesterday. Jenny was always receiving calls at the eleventh hour to help somebody out of a jam.

Jenny sat up in her bed abruptly as she tried to distance herself from the uncomfortable dream and make sense of the weird feeling that she was not alone in her home. As she began to focus, Jenny realized that she was not alone. Carefully she wiped the last remnants of sleep from her eyes and stared at a warm energy field that she just knew was from heaven. The messenger from God called Jenny by her entire name, Jennifer Ellen Baxter, in a voice that was crystal clear. She knew in her heart without a doubt that no mistake had been made regarding this visit.

The messenger confirmed that he has been sent by God to deliver a personal message to Jenny. God had decided to give Jenny a rarely done advance notice of her departure from earth. The messenger said that she had three days left on earth with two conditions. God wants you to be very clear about the Ten Commandments. If you break any one of the Commandments at any time during the three days before I return for you, your spirit will be dispatched straight to hell at a speed twice that of light. Jenny began to think, twice the speed of light and commented out loud, "Whoa, that means that I could go from earth to hell in almost no time at all. That's incredible." Not incredible, we call it Godspeed. That is why God's angels are never late when conducting His business. Secondly, you cannot tell anyone the conditions of God's plan. If you do, you will be cut off from the Spirit of God.

You will not be able to think or utter God's name or the name of Christ Jesus ever again.

Jenny looked at her calendar as her heart raced madly and she realized that time suddenly took on a whole new significance in her life. Jenny began to think about her short term plans. She had to prioritize the most important thing on her "to do" list that 10th day of September 2001. The notice from Heaven caused her to think about the seasons in a different light. Jenny's time on earth was down to three days and counting. Jenny began to think about winter. As the thought settled into her mind, Jenny knew that the memories of last winter would be the last winter that she would experience on earth. The thought continued to the seasons of the spring and summer. Jenny realized the significance of the seasons and the reason that the days flow as they do. Another thought occurred to her, one day at a time. How many times had Jenny heard one of God's children say, one day at a time Sweet Jesus, tomorrow may not be mine. Give me the strength, give me the sense to take one day at a time.

Jenny became stressed about the first thing she should do. Should she concern herself with making sure that her will was accurate and up to date. Should she make a list of the people that she wanted to hug and tell how much she loved them. Jenny wondered if she had time to travel and to where. It seemed as if the minutes were rushing by like seconds.

Jenny feel a tightness in her chest as she wondered, do I know all of the Commandments as well as I should to get me through the next three days without making a mistake that will cause time to stop for me. Should she take her Bible with her or would she have enough time to do some reading now. Jenny heard an echo in her mind of a loved one saying, you really should read your Bible more often. Jenny wondered if she should have talked to God more often than her usual two times a day. In the mornings, Jenny always remembered to thank Him for waking her up for another day. Jenny was consistent at night for thanking God for the blessings He gave her that day.

Jenny wondered if she had time to throw one last pity party for herself as she looked back on her life. She began to tear up at the thought of the times that she was embarrassed by her mistakes, the moments of emotional stress caused by bad decisions because of youthful immaturity on her part. Only if she had known then what she knew now. Jenny could only imagine how different things might have been. It dawned on Jenny that walking down the road of life was not meant to be peachy and rosy all the time. This world is not a perfect place. There were good and bad days for a reason. Jenny remembered that it was hard to do the right thing sometimes but it was not impossible. Her faith in the fact that Jesus was always there for her made a huge difference when she was struggling through difficult times.

Jenny thought about how tired she was after running around trying to tie up loose ends. She checked the calendar to verify the time she had left. Unbelievably the calendar read September 12 and it is 11 pm already. How can that be. Sometime time flies but this is madness. So little time left with so much to do. Her mind began to whirl and her body felt as if giant weights were on both of her shoulders. Trying to cope in a rational manner in this situation seemed like an impossible mission. Jenny thought back and said,

"Wait a minute. I didn't ask to be born in the first place. I may have made some poor choices when selecting some of the roads that I have traveled. I accept responsibility for that. I know that I didn't travel with the best of companions on some occasions during my youth. I accept responsibility for that. This situation is squeezing me from all sides and there is nothing that I can do about it. I am so weary and my very soul feels tired right now. Dear Lord, I wish you could help me in my time of need.

Jenny rolled over and noticed that her nightshirt was damp from perspiration and she was breathing hard. The clock read 3 a.m., September 11, 2001. It was early Tuesday morning and she felt the slight throb of a headache. Jenny tried with all of her might to focus on her surroundings. She was at home in her very familiar and comfortable bed. Jenny had been tossing and turning most of the night. She was greatly relieved to wake up from one of the worst dreams of her life. Jenny sat up on the edge of the bed and decided to get another nightshirt. She decided to get a few more hours of much needed sleep and treat herself to the best breakfast in the world.

Jenny reflected on how difficult and challenging life can be sometimes. She thought to herself, I am so glad that God is in control and He has a Master plan for this world that we pass through. Trying to deal with the knowledge that she only had three days and counting before she would have leave this earth was torturous and almost unbearable. She wondered at what point near the end would she just shut down completely and watch the time ebb away as she tried to visualize mortal death.

Jenny thanked God for Jesus with the comfort in knowing that He will get me through the rest of this day on September 11 and the rest of my days according to God's Will. She finally drifted off to a much needed restful sleep with the echo of THY WILL be done on earth as It is in heaven floating in her mind.

Jenny woke up later that morning and was having a cup of coffee in bed as she watched the morning news. It was just before 9 AM when the news anchorman began talking about a breaking news report in New York City. There was an early report of a plane accident at one of the World Trade Center Towers. Jenny found her attention glued to the television set for most of the day as she absorbed the unfolding events on that historic day.

Most people who lived through September 11, 2001 would remember that day as the ATTACK ON AMERICA. September 11, 2001 contained extra-ordinary events that impacted our nation in a historical way that joins it to monumental historical moments in time. If one were to freeze a frame of one's mortal life at any moment, one would notice that all living individuals share the same unique situation. At any giving frozen moment in our life-time, we are caught between coming and going. We had no say in when, where or how we were born. Most of us will have no say in when, where or how we will leave this earth.

Some philosophers have compared a man's life "LIKE THE SAND THROUGH AN HOUR GLASS so are the days of our lives." On the cosmic scale of time, a man's life has been likened to a twenty-four hour day. A man's birth is his **dawn**. He grows through the **morning**, **noon** and **evening**. Man dies at his **mid-night**.

Many spiritual people, regardless of their religious belief, view life on earth similar to the tip of an iceberg. You can easily see what extends above the water line but you also know that a portion of the iceberg extends below the surface of the water. A newborn individual is tagged with a DOB (date of birth) when they arrive in the world. A review of history has very effectively shown that a DOD (date of departure) from this earth is linked to each person. There are no known exceptions to this natural law and there is no getting around it. History has also shown that many people have a very strong belief that life extends beyond the exit point of this mortal world.

THE BUS
STOP MYSTERY

It was a normal sight for the six friends, Earl Wiley, Karen Pearlman, Carl Fellows, Nancy Dain, Mildred O'Bannon and Richard Samples, to be seen seated at their favorite table by the window for the late dinner. A soft gentle rain fell outside as the staff worker, Eugene Talbot, sat in the chair usually occupied by Earl Wiley and explained why Mr. Wiley was absent from his usual place at the dinner table. Mr. Wiley was frequently called "the little old man". The name was given to him by some of the younger residents at the Golden Years Retirement Villa many years ago. It was 7:15 p.m. on that somber Monday evening that five of the usual six members of the late evening dinner group listened to the details of Eugene's afternoon experience.

Eugene was thoroughly briefed on "the little old man's" normal bus stop routine on his first day of employment at the Golden Years Retirement Villa seventeen years ago. The five dinner companions remembered the many times "the little old man" said that he was the last surviving member of his family and childhood friends. All of them had been called home ahead of him over a period of years during the latter part of his life. The only reminders he had left were a few pictures and fading memories in his mind of his past. The friends at the table knew that he was a retired military man. They admired his daily spotless manner of dress and the orderly condition of his living quarters.

It was sometime after his 71st birthday that "the little old man" began walking to the bus stop three blocks away from the Golden Years Retirement Villa on Kings Highway and Central Avenue every afternoon. He left the Villa and arrived at the bus stop a little before 3 p.m. and would sit on the bench until 6:30 p.m. At 6:30 p.m., "the little old man" would look at his watch, pick up his little black leather case and walk back to the Villa for the late evening dinner.

During the first three months of his daily walk to the bus stop, he was routinely asked, "Where are you going today?" "The little old man's" reply became standard and predictable. "I am going to wait on my bus that will take me home." From time to time, some people asked, "What's in the black case?" "The little old man" would say, "I have everything that I need in this case."

After the first four months of his bus stop routine, the regular bus drivers, cab operators and police officers noticed the visible absence of "the little old man" on Sunday afternoons. The regular bus riders would ask about him a minute after 3 p.m., if he wasn't seated on the bench in his spot next to the glass wall of the bus stop shelter. The weather rarely kept "the little old man" away from the bus stop. On the rare occasions when the weather was very uncomfortable for the mail carriers, police officers, fire fighters, trash collectors, Fed-Ex and U.P.S. drivers, "the little old man" would postpone his trip until the following day.

"The little old man" began using a walking cane after his 86th birthday to make his Monday through Saturday walk to the bus stop. By the time his 91st birthday came around he had spent the major portion of twenty years of his afternoons at the bus stop. Occasional attacks of sinus headaches and low back muscle aches caused "the little old man" to cancel his normal trip to the bus stop. As usual on Monday at 3:01 p.m. when "the little old man" was not seated in his spot on the bench, the question was asked. "Have you seen "the little old man" today? One of the residents told Eugene that he had not seen Mr. Earl since the previous Saturday evening.

Eugene knocked on the door several times before he used the pass key to enter "the little old man's room. Eugene found him still in bed at 4:30 p.m. Mr. Earl appeared to be sleeping very peacefully at first glance. Everything in the room seemed to be in its place. Eugene soon realized that "the little old man" was sleeping too peacefully and he was not breathing. Eugene notified Sandra Hodges, the Retirement Villa administrator, and the staff doctor, Ben Kildare. Dr. Kildare was familiar with the peaceful look of sleep on Mr. Earl's face, but his professional experience quickly confirmed that "the little old man" had been called home.

As the trio looked down on "the little old man" they saw his black leather case and his walking cane on the floor adjacent to the head of his bed. For several moments they gazed at the case in total silence. No one said a word. Ms. Hodges walked over to the small leather case and opened it. Dr. Kildare and Eugene asked at the same time, "What's in it?" Ms. Hodges answered them in a hushed voice, " I don't see anything in it. It's empty."

Richard said, "Things won't be the same around here without Mr. Earl. I can't believe that he is gone. I started eating with him about twelve years ago. My meals were dull without him on the few occasions that "the little old man" was sick in his room. Richard laughed for a brief moment. "The little old man" used to say that the walk from the bus stop gave him a hearty appetite.

Nancy said that she remembered asking "the little old man" one time if he had heard the song from the south regarding the sweet chariot swinging down to carry people home. You know how Mr. Earl constantly read books and magazines and listened to his talk show on the radio. "The little old man" had a vast knowledge concerning a lot of subjects. Mr. Earl told me the history behind the song. He said that "Swing down Sweet Chariot" was a Negro spiritual song that was sung by the people in the south who were forced to pick cotton in the cotton fields in the days of slavery from sun-up to sundown.

Mildred said that she discussed her favorite song, "People Get Ready" by the Impressions with Mr. Earl. The message by the Impressions referred to a train moving from coast to coast picking up passengers for the ride to "Glory" to be with God. There was no need for baggage or tickets. "Faith" was only thing needed by the passengers to hear the humming diesel engines and board the train.

Karen said, "Mr. Earl's mind was as sharp as a tack." A couple of weeks ago, he told me about a minister's version of the three companions and their blind friend. The minister delivered an excellent sermon after asking the question, "Who prayed for you?" The ministered wanted to know if anyone in the congregation

53

knew the name of the person whose prayers brought them to Jesus for salvation.

The minister used the example of the three friends who delivered their blind friend at the feet of Jesus to be healed. In short, Jesus was preaching in a crowded temple one Sunday morning and there was standing room only at the rear of the temple, when the three friends arrived with their blind companion. The three friends took their blind companion to the roof of the temple, made a hole in the roof and the four of them came crashing down at the foot of Jesus in the middle of his sermon. The minister said that the friends knew how to make an entrance. Jesus looked at the friends and said, "By the commitment of your faith, I forgive your sins." Jesus restored the sight of the blind companion.

Carl said, "Mr. Earl was so kind and gentle. I wonder if he really caught his bus to go home?"

Mildred reminded Carl of a favorite saying by Mr. Earl. Jesus said, "Anything is possible with God." God knows that Mr. Earl really believed that one day he would catch his bus at that stop. I can only imagine the happiness at the reunion with "the little old man" and his family members and friends on the other side.

The other friends at the table with tear filled eyes agreed and said, "Yeah, what a happy thought."

A View from Below
(What the Devil Might Say About It)

The amount of knowledge available to the average person has increased dramatically with access to computers, cell phones and entertainment systems to an incredible degree. Wouldn't it be interesting to listen in on the thoughts of the devil and his view of the younger generation.

Why should He get the Glory? Somewhere in the Bible it states that He created a universe at the utterance of His voice. Is that such a grand feat for God? After all God is almighty. If I had His power I could have done it and probably would have done it anyway. Why should He get the Glory for that. Some scientists have been trying to figure out for years how He created the universe. To date, there is no valid explanation that will satisfy them. It reminds me of the round earth issue. Once upon a time some folk thought the earth was flat (my kind of thinkers). The opposing opinion claimed that the earth was round. A few bold sailors and their fact seeking friends eventually convinced the others that the earth was round. Does it really matter to anyone that God gives some scientist extraordinary intelligence to make their search for an explanation of how He did it more interesting. Folk like Einstein and his other busy body friends were able to validate the theories of the scientists who came before them.

The launching of the Hubble Space Telescope (HST) has rewritten the books on astrology and confirmed the fact that the universe is really very large. Photos from the HST have shown that the size of the universe is bigger than the earlier estimates of some astrologists who were thought to have been missing a few of their light bulbs during their time.

Yeah, why should He get the Glory for the eternity plan of His? He is the only one that can understand it. It is more complicated than playing chess on a twenty-four dimensional level. He makes all the rules. My plans are foiled so many times. I believe He makes rules as His plan goes along. What sense does it make to give each of His children a soul with the same value before they are actually birthed in the world. Under the present economic monetary system, a conservative estimate of the value of a soul would be about a billion dollars. Who would have thought that? Hold on, it gets better. The new owner of a soul does not get to discuss the net worth of their soul with a financial planner before or after birth. A great many of them never realize what a valuable piece of real estate their soul is and I just love it. There are some fine print rules in His soul deal that drives me crazy.

God made some commandments (about ten I think) and He insisted that His followers obey each one. In addition to a soul, God thought it wise to give them "free will" also. Come on, be for real. God starts you out with a soul that has a conservative value of a billion dollars, gives you "free will" and He expects you to follow His rules if you want to or not. I have to say God is good about giving each of His children unconditional love and plenty of opportunities to ask for forgiveness for their sins. I know I would not have been so generous. This one is really good if you are ready. God said that a person needs to get daily bread in order to live. One can get the daily bread by reading the Bible. My rule for daily bread would be to spread a hot taco sauce or salsa topping on your bread before you eat it. The hotter the sauce, the better the thrill. The value of the soul has to be validated before you finish your last mile of your visit on earth. A lot of people miss the boat on this one. It really makes me laugh that so few have figured out that the last mile is measured backward. When you take your last step on earth, that is it.

God makes the schedule concerning who comes and who goes. This rule has been around longer than I have. Some of His children are a riot when they get the call from Him to come home. They acted so shocked by the call. What, my time is up already? They look around and desperately start begging for a little more time to do some of the things that He wanted them to because they spent all of their time doing their own thing. The soul must be validated by Christ Jesus before the child's time on earth ends. It seems like a weird rule to the lazy ones who don't read the Bible, go to church or listen to the message at funerals. I can not get enough of them, my kind of folk.

I could never understand this scene. The child enters the world crying. The family members are full of joy and happiness. Some take pictures, buy gifts and throw little parties. This child has to go through the toil and trials of the earth experience like all of those in the family line before him. The new arrival will have to deal with hunger, being cold, catching colds, childhood ailments and growing up, and trying to resist my temptations (I love having my fun).

Kindergarten in most cases is not too bad of a deal. They have to survive the first grade and school homework until the education process is over. When the faithful have spent their time on earth and get the call from God to leave, usually they are happy and delighted to know that they have no need for tears and are headed for mo better days. Some have questions and concerns about the ones they are leaving behind. Those concerns are quickly laid to rest with the assurance that God takes care of His own always.

The family members and close friends gather at the news of one's mortal death with much weeping and words of sorrow. You would think that they would be cheering wildly, jumping for joy and celebrating more than they did at the birth of a child saying, "Yeah, another one has made it out of here. Let's have a cook out."

The validated soul is the passport to a lifestyle in heaven that only God knows what it is like. A validated soul at the time of mortal death is simply **priceless**. Once I get your soul, I would not sell it back to you for two billion dollars. If you offer to buy it back, I would laugh at you and say, "Show me the money. You don't have a dollar. Everything you had in the world really belonged to God."

Hang on to your hats. I have been able to use a line that causes people to part with their souls for an exchange rate that is criminal. That is how I get my thrills. Why should you waste your time on earth by following the rules, working hard being decent, being caring, giving respect to other people when you can have a hot time with me for eternity. You can spend your days bending and breaking the rules to your satisfaction. Put a new spin on chaos and a different twist on confusion. When God tells them that their time on earth is up, I give new meaning to the phrase used on the "Price is Right" show, **come on down**. Those who think they like it really hot are in for a surprise when they make it to my hangout. Many say, "wow it is hot as hell in here." I tell them that this is the refrigerated section for them to lose their chill. It gets much much better than this little warm up drill. I love doing business with the ignorant. They are so good at taking short cuts and dodging responsibility. They know all of the excuses. They keep me updated with the new ones. They are so good at making up excuses as they go along. Some of them crave the drug scene. Getting high on natural life and the wonders created by God does not work for them.

God's request, to love thy neighbor as thyself, has been a source of great entertainment for me for years. I have laughed at so many of you who have struggled with this concept when dealing with some of your blood relatives. We won't even go into mentioning love thy neighbor. There are mind staggering numbers of you who have trouble dealing with yourself at times. Especially when you (as it's called now-a-days) are "having a moment".

My favorite people figure that something is wrong with God's deal. This deal is too good to be true. Why should God be concerned with my soul. On one occasion while responding to Job's questions in the Bible, God said, "Everything above and beneath the heavens belongs to me." At one point some of God's children were doing so poorly with the "free will" gift that He gave them in his original plan. God gave them a Savior to guarantee their chance to enjoy eternal life.

God wanted His namesake to be the King of kings. I guess some people have a hard time grasping the concept that the King of kings could be born in a barn, placed in a manger and have the authority to validate a soul for eternal acceptance. Maybe it is the eternity part that they can not comprehend. Perhaps it could be the one star thing. They seem to forget that God makes the rules.

If I were putting on the show, I would have chose Las Vegas for the birth place of my son and lit up the place with twice as many lights as there are in Vegas today. Thinking like that and my wanting to have God's job is probably what got me kicked out of heaven with some of my followers. I am still looking for a few good people with high intelligence, who are willing to help me win the battle over good and righteousness.

You can read in the Bible for yourself where Jesus, the King of kings told a wealthy man to give away his riches and follow Him on earth for a greater reward of riches in heaven. The man refused the offer. I knew then that he was stuck on stupid. A high five for another live one. His big vision was to spend it while he had it, my man. He just couldn't see giving it away. The concept, it is better to give than to receive, just did not work for him. Again, why should God get the Glory? His namesake dedicated the Lord's Prayer to Him. Do you know how many times that prayer has been recited? You can't begin to imagine such a number in your mind. Einstein couldn't either.

Just like the Perfect Son. Following the Heavenly Father's example. His followers call him the Best Friend, the Lamb of God, the Peacemaker and the Light of the world to name a few. What happened to the sun and moon? The Bible refers to the sun as the light of the day and the moon as the light of the night. What was that all about? All I get is wise sayings, "The devil made me do it. Damn the devil and the one phrase repeated too often, that damned devil." Why can't they just say the devil may have set it up but I made the choice.

It is difficult for the new generation with the credit cards, microwave ovens, giant screen color televisions, walkman radios and cell phones to get on board with an honest day's work for a day's pay. They would rather have it now and let somebody else pay for it later. Some of them are content to live with thier parents until they hit the lottery, collect social security or the parents disown or evict them. What is this world coming to?

Again why should God get the Glory? He has done so much to make it possible for the faithful to enjoy eternal life in heaven with Him and Christ Jesus. What about the one who will come upon judgement day and discover that their name is not in the book of life? There is no bad day on earth that can prepare you for the depth of disappointment to learn that you did not make the count. The worst month of days that you can imagine now will not begin to compare to the pain that will grip your heart and soul in less than a moment at the announcement of the judgement that you are hell bound. It will be a sad sight for some and a thrill for me to see them pleading with the angel to check under place in the book of life for their name? Please, please, please check under "round to it". The angel's reply, "Why should I check under 'round to it"? Because I was planning on getting my soul validated as soon as I could get around to it. I'll bet you will find their name under "Going Down, please".

The Lord knew what He was doing when he made your smile and voice. Be generous in letting Him see and hear both of them more often. The Lord is my Shepherd. If you don't know what a Great Friend Jesus is, I urge you to find out soon.

Interview with
the Devil

Devil. Greetings, you are the new arrival. Clyde, right.

New arrival. Are you the devil?

Devil. Yes I am. Why do you ask?

Clyde. I want to be sure that I am speaking to the head man this time. What in the hell am I doing down here?

Devil. Are you a comedian?

Clyde. No, I am not. Thank you.

Devil. We do have a few rules down here. 1st rule. That is the last time you can crack the hell joke down here. If I had a penny for every time I have heard that comment. I would have more money than God.

Clyde. Oh yeah, why is that?

Devil. Ask one of the few jokers inside who tried using that line for the second time down here. You will surely run into one or two while you are here. You may get lucky and run into Flathead. He cracked the forbidden joke twice. A real slow learner that one.

Clyde. What happened to him?

Devil. I don't know. I haven't seen him in the last three thousand years.

Clyde. Three thousand years. How long will I be here?

Devil. What did they tell you upstairs?

Clyde. You mean the old guy. St. Peter, his name was St. Peter. I told him that I wanted to speak to God. The old man said that I should have talked to Him when I was on earth.

Interested the Devil asked, "What did you say then Clyde?"

Clyde. Well I was truthful. I told St. Peter that I didn't have time to talk to God when I was on earth. I slipped up and talked about him on occasions when things were going bad for me but I wasn't alone, a lot of other folk did it too.

Devil. Oh, you don't have to tell me. You will see most of them inside.

Clyde. St. Peter wouldn't even hook me up with a short rap session with JC. What's up with that? He told me to take the elevator marked down. I asked him again, "How long will I be down there. St. Peter said that only God knows.

Devil. Well Clyde. That is the answer to your question. Only God knows. There are only a few rules down here. It is my job to go over them with you personally. You see I had to keep tabs on you while you were on earth. I had an interest in making sure that your slide on the road to hell was lubricated with plenty of temptations. Now that you are here with me, I'll see you from time to time when I see you.

Clyde. Man, that is cold blooded wrong Mr. D.

Devil. We have a no work rule down here.

Clyde. Thinking to himself. A no work rule. Things are looking up. This just might be my kind of a set-up. "I am curious. Who made that rule?"

Devil. God made that rule. As always He likes to have the last word on everything. Even on my turf in hell.

Clyde. How often does God come down here? Clyde was thinking that maybe he might get a chance to talk to God on one of His visits.

Devil. God has only been here once since He kicked me down here. He wanted to check out the heat level. That brings me to another rule. We have double heat days on the weekends. God does have a sense of humor. He thought it would give us variety and a way to tell when the weekend was coming. The temperature of the heat is doubled on the weekend. God did that.

I don't allow comments such as hot as hell.

I am in one hell of a mess.

Certainly no, what in the hell am I doing here comments.

If you don't know by now, you will never know.

Clyde. Well if there is a no work rule, what in the h.

The Devil shot Clyde a look that cooked his thought as he was speaking.

Clyde. Oops, my bad. It won't happen again. What do people do down here?

Devil. Well you get to talk to each other about how hot it is but you can't make jokes about the heat. You see when I am down here on the weekends, I get to feel the heat as well. Saturdays and Sundays are no picnic days in here.

Clyde. So you are telling me there is no way out of here?

Devil. Well if there is, only God knows. He made the elevator that only comes down and let people off. I don't know how God did it. I guess it is similar to that creating the soul trick of His. A soul can't be duplicated and no one has come close to imitating one.

Until God holds His judgement day, I can come and go as I please. God does have the two hour rule.

Clyde. You have my complete undivided attention. Lay the two hour rule on me man.

Devil. If you can go for a 100 years without ever thinking about getting out of here, God has a special arrangement. Permanent guest here are granted a two hour visit to Death Valley in the hottest part of the afternoon to watch the snakes crawling by on the sand.

Clyde. What kind of a deal is that?

Devil. Think about it. It gives one a chance to reflect on "free will". You will get a chance to experience a twinkling of the pain that God feels when He watches one of His children slowly drifting to the dark side on earth and by sinning their way to hell.

Clyde. I have to tell you right now. This is not going to work for me. I need to speak to God right now.

Devil. Looking at Clyde in wonderment. Clyde, I know that paying attention in school wasn't your strong suit. Son, you have to accept your situation. You couldn't speak to God when you were in Heaven.

There are no telephones, no cell phones, beepers, wide screen TVs, portable TVs, small screen TVs or loud speakers. You won't find a telegram station, newspaper, post card, writing paper or a bottle down here. How in the hell do you think you can speak to God anytime when you get good and ready?

You are truly in hell. That is a hot fact of reality. You have one of two choices.

You can get over it.

Or you can get used to it. The choice is yours.

Clyde. You may as well tell me what's off limits down here. I would hate to step out of bounds and have to spend time in "time out." Clyde added quickly, I didn't mean that as a hellish joke Mr. D.

Devil. God is Good about the security arrangement. You can go anywhere you want. There seems to be no end to hell and the **dang blasted heat** is everywhere.

Clyde your interview is over. Tell the next sinner to come on in.

Wait Right Here

Marlow walked over to the Angel at the door. "Are you the Angel who can show me where I need to go?"

Angel. Were you sent here by St. Peter?

Marlow. Yes I was.

Angel. There is something wrong with your soul. You will have to wait in line to talk to God to see if you will be allowed in Heaven.

Marlow. Why do I have to wait in line to talk to God? When I was on earth, I could talk to God whenever I got ready.

Angel. Well, you are not on earth. Your soul doesn't have that Heavenly glow. Do you know how many years God waited on you every day to talk to Him?

Marlow. No, right off the top of my head, I don't know.

Angel. When was the last time you talked to God?

Marlow. I am a little ashamed. It has been awhile.

Angel. Go through this door and take you place at the end of the line to make an appointment to talk to God.

Please beware of the rules and make sure that you obey them.

There is no line jumping.

You can not save a place for someone if they decide to get out of line.

You can get out of line whenever you decide.

If you get on the elevator marked **"Going down, please".** It works just one way. It will take you down but it will not bring you up.

Marlow stepped through the door and was immediately greeted by the sweetest smelling breeze he had ever experienced. The wide expanse of carpet green grass was the truest green Marlow had ever seen. He saw the end of a long line and began walking toward it.

Marlow walked for hours it seemed. He finally arrived at the end of the line.

He was standing near the top of a hill. There was a snaking line of people that meandered across the beautiful green landscape as far as he could see.

Marlow. Man this is a long line to get into Heaven.

Sanford was the last person in line ahead of Marlow. He said, "Correction my brother. This is the line to make an appointment with the calendar Angel to get a reservation to talk to God about your possibility of getting into Heaven."

Marlow. Get out. All of these people are waiting to make an appointment to talk to God. This seems so unfair. When I was on earth, I could have talked to God anytime.

Sanford. I don't think you can imagine the number of people on God's good list up here that want to talk to him.

By the way, how well do you know Jesus?

Marlow. Who me? I, I uh, I uh, uh.

Sanford. You do know where you are don't you. The only thing that comes out up here is the truth. The whole truth and nothing but the truth.

Marlow. I, I, I uh know that's right.

Sanford. It sounds like you came mighty close to getting that infamous one way elevator ride **"going down, please"**.

Marlow. I will admit, I was very nervous and worried about where I would end up. I was a middle of the roader on earth.

Sanford. You don't say. I tried to stay in the middle of the road myself. I had no interest in all that hocus pocus boogey man stuff.

I will be honest with you. I had a hard time trying to visualize living past 120 years anywhere. When I pondered on the subject, I gave up when I got to the thought of being seventy years old on earth.

I said, "Just let me die and get it over with."

Marlow. How fast does this line move anyway?

Sanford. I really don't know. It just seems to get longer and longer. If you get out of line to look around, you have to go to the end of the line.

Marlow. Yes, I know. I got the speech. How far have you moved?

Sanford. Not much but I have met a lot of people. My situation is a carryover from earth I guess. I never was a patient person. It bothers me to stand around doing nothing. I have been in and out of line about eighty times.

Marlow. You are kidding. You got out of line EIGHTY times. Why?

Sanford. Look, after standing in one spot without moving, I had to look around.

Marlow. How long did you stand in one spot.

Sanford. I couldn't tell you. Up here, there is no time.

Marlow. Man, this is a whole lot different than being on earth.

My time ran out down there like a wink and a blink. I had no 2 minute warning, no bells or whistles.

I woke up one morning dead. My body was laying there like a door nail.

It was a very weird experience for awhile. I thought I was going to panic.

I remembered somewhere THEY said, "Follow the light, follow the light."

At one point some shadowy figures tried to get me to come to them.

Sanford. That same thing happened to me. I didn't go because I thought they would grab me and drag down to hell.

Clarence T. was standing in line ahead of Sanford. He said, "I could not help overhearing some of your conversation.

I used to wake up at night, drenched in sweat because I was trying to get away from the dark figures that were trying to drag me to hell while I was sleeping.

I hung out with the "In crowd" at least that was what I thought.

Their flawed logic caught up with me. Some of them believed that they came from nowhere.

They planned to live their lives in a way to get the biggest bang for their buck. They figured that when they died. That would be that and no consequences. The last laugh will be on them.

Marlow. I thought that way for awhile. In my case the "reap what you sow" theory kept creeping into my mind. Especially when I attended somebody's funeral. Eventually the ministers' messages sank in.

I have heard of too many tales of horror from people who lived their lives any old way and always seemed to be in the pit, as compared to the few carefree individuals who seemed to get away with murder.

Clarence T. Yes there seemed to be very few cases of real happiness in the non believers that I knew. Most of them were into drinking, using drugs, involved in heavy gambling, trying to find a way to beat the system or get into devil worship.

Sanford. I had to question their sense of balance. How could they believe in evil and the devil and not consider that God was real.

I will be the first one to admit that it took a long time for the light to flick on in my head. I never had a doubt in my mind when it came to evil. I knew that I was not getting into anything that involved the devil.

Clarence T. I can tell you for a fact that I was thrown for a double loop when I first heard that someone read in the Bible that God created evil.

That bit of news put a chill in my jeans and caused me to do some serious thinking about my future.

If God created evil and I had seen plenty of evidence to know that evil was real, I asked myself, "How can evil win the battle of good versus evil?"

Marlow. I wasn't born to be a rocket scientist but it doesn't take a genius to know that the odds in that battle are against the devil, big time.

I should have made a stronger commitment sooner to be on God's side in the war for souls.

Only a fool would chose to be on the losing team if he had a choice.

Sanford. The theory of being born on earth just to die did not ring up a lot of points for me. The lack of logic in the theory of from nothing to nothing just did not add up for me.

Marlow. Has anyone here ever been on a cruise?

I have heard some people say that being on a very good cruise is like a sneak preview of Heaven. A five or seven day cruise on a luxury ship.

Clarence T. I have heard about some of the experiences of several of my friends who have taken luxury cruises.

They did tend to rant and rave about the endless opportunities to eat delicious meals, enjoy excellent stage entertainment and a variety of exciting social events. They said that they had the time of their lives.

It made me rethink my position of the eternity theory and whether or not I wanted to be included in that number. Just imagine, to live forever.

Marlow. The twins, Chaos and Confusion tried to recruit me to their way of thinking. They started out with a tempting sale in the beginning. There was a time when I considered raising "h" and just living it up and never mind the rules.

The end game of Chaos and Confusion did not work for me.

I wondered what would happen if they won. Who would be in charge.

Sanford. I would be wondering who would be in competition for the devil's job if they won.

You know once upon a time in Heaven, the devil decided that he wanted God's job.

James Douglas was standing in line in front of Clarence T.

James Douglas. Yeah, what you are saying makes sense. On earth, I noticed that most of the people I knew wanted someone else's job. They always wanted to move up.

Some had egos so big, they wanted to replace Jesus Christ. Can you believe that?

Sanford. As I was saying, I could not see trying to out do somebody's evil deed just to be a member of the devil's club.

I decided to stay in the middle of the road and play it safe for awhile longer. I didn't want to take a position either way.

Clarence T. What caused me to cross over was when I wondered what would it be like if a mansion was made by God.

Think about it. There are so many amazing natural wonders on earth and so little time to see them all.

I began to give some serious thought about the eternity theory.

It sounded too good to be true in the beginning. I began to look backward at the universe, the age of the earth and the progress of the living conditions of man.

It started to dawn on me that the passage of time has been a planned phenomenon.

Marlow. It would take an enormous amount of time to experience all of the wonders on earth. Only God knows how much time it would take for someone to experience and enjoy all of the wonders He has prepared for his faithful children in Heaven.

Thomas was standing in front of James Douglas.

Thomas. You fellas have got a mighty interesting conversation going.

I was a very important man on earth. I owned my own chain of barbecue restaurants. I spent most of my time and my life building that business from scratch. I guess you could say that I was a workaholic.

The business got so big, I didn't have time for anything else.

I gave food and money to the homeless and the local charities.

I failed to take time to talk to God. Yes, I said, "Thank God" from time to time. I didn't take time to talk to Him and make a commitment of getting my soul saved.

Clarence T. began to chuckle a couple of times.

He chuckled a couples of more times. He was trying not to laugh.

He began laughing and couldn't stop. He managed to say that he heard that God had a sense of humor.

They others joined Clarence T. in laughing for a short time.

Clarence T. Finally said, "Wouldn't it be funny if God has got us standing in this line to make up for all the time He waited to talk to us and we didn't show up."

Oh, oh, oh, I can't take it. You reap what you sow theory is like a boomerang. It really does come back around.

The others slowly stopped laughing and began to look at each other. Then they looked ahead at that long, long, long, long line.

Thomas. If I reap what I sowed, I will be standing in this line for a very long time just to make an appointment to talk to God.

Man, I wish I had known on earth what seems to be dawning on me now.

Marlow. Me too brother. I wasted some valuable time on earth doing little pitley things.

Thomas. Clarence T., did you do a lot of praying?

Clarence T. Man no. I never prayed. If it were not for bad luck, I would not have had any luck on earth. I was too busy pulling on my bootstraps to get myself out of one bad situation after another.

Sanford. That reminds me our of time on earth.

OUR TIME ON EARTH

Time on earth is finite,

Ticking seconds flee by with amazing speed.

There are sixty seconds in a minute.

Once that minute has passed, you can never get it back.

Sixty minutes are in an hour.

Hours streak by at the same speed as seconds.

Only hours do it, one minute at a time to be exact.

Time has been around on earth for many years.

In each individual case it seems that time is in short supply.

Especially when you are using the time of someone else.

Sometimes while they are waiting for you,

Whether the minutes speed or creep by.

It seems like they are waiting to die.

How much time each one has on earth,

Only our Heavenly Father knows.

Marlow. Sanford that was really deep. It reminds me of when I used to think about "nothing".

J.D. What do you mean thinking about nothing. I have heard reputed scientists say that it is impossible to think about nothing. You are always thinking about something. Even if you are sleep.

Marlow. Not for me. You are wrong. I did it quite a bit.

I started out by concentrating on nothing. After awhile, I got pretty good at it.

Teachers in school would ask me, "Marlow, what are you thinking about?"

I would answer them truthfully, "Nothing."

J.D. Marlow, you did waste some serious time on earth. I am glad that I am in line ahead of you.

Clarence T. Just standing in this line is almost as bad as being in hell.

THUNDER IN THE BACKGROUND

People all up and the down the line were looking around and mumbling, "Who said the 'h' word?"

J.D. Clarence trust me on this one. You don't want to even think the "h" word up here.

I can assure you that you don't even want to think about being in line to go that place, let alone actually be there.

Marlow. My grandmother would tell us all the time, "God ain't somebody to play with. You had better watch your mouth."

J.D. Have you heard about the joke the devil has been playing for his homeboys?

Clarence T. No. I haven't.

J.D. The devil tells them that they can go anywhere they want in "h" to find satisfaction.

Clarence T. What's so funny about that?

Sanford. They can never find satisfaction down there because satisfaction is inside of heaven.

J.D. They can't tell jokes down there but the devil lets them sing just one song.

Marlow. OK, I'll bite on this one. Which one song can they sing down below?

J.D. and Sanford. (Singing together) I can't seem to find my satisfaction.

I can't seem to find my satisfaction.

I have searched all over and I have tried.

I can't find my satisfaction. Oh, no I just can't find it.

RUNNING OUT OF TIME

TABLE OF CONTENTS

Chapter 1   The Traffic Stop 82

Chapter 2   The Drug Task Force 87

Chapter 3   The South Beach Crowd 90

Chapter 4   Ricardo's Confession 93

Chapter 5   Jack's Bombshell 96

Chapter 6   The Magic Man 98

Chapter 7   Night Flight 102

Chapter 8   Interrupted Sleep 107

Chapter 9   Bad News 110

Chapter 10 Sanchez's Vow of Revenge 114

Chapter 11 The Devil's Man 119

Chapter 12 Drake's Wild Card 122

Chapter 13 The Tick of the Clock 126

Chapter 14 The Set-up 132

Chapter 15 Free Lunch 139

Chapter 16 Everybody's Talking 144

Chapter 17 Sarah's Call 149

Chapter ONE

Ricardo Avilla was cruising along at 65 MPH in his sleek Mercedes Benz listening to Latin Jazz Greats and formulating a plan to follow his Uncle Sanchez's advice regarding their financial situation. Ricardo was about twenty minutes away from his Miami estate-styled fortress when he noticed the red and blue flashing light in his rear view mirror. Ricardo pulled over to see why he was being stopped.

Officer Jack Daniels was working a traffic detail on the evening shift on June 21, 2001 thinking about his upcoming week-end off when he realized the black Mercedes ahead of him was driving at a constant 10 MPH over the posted speed limit of 55 MPH. Officer Daniels wasn't interested in logging out on a traffic stop because he was not pulling this driver over for a Driving Under the Influence (DUI) field sobriety check. Officer Daniels was going to caution the driver on his speed and let him go. An internal warning told Officer Daniels to record the vehicle tag number and a description of the car on his computer note pad. Officer Daniels knew that he was deviating from the proper officer safety rule but a fudged note would be better than no information if something went terribly wrong.

As Officer Daniels was walking toward Ricardo, the driver was nervously thinking about the half a million dollars in US currency in the trunk of his car. Ricardo did not need this complication in his life.

Officer Daniels asked, "May I see your driver's license and the vehicle registration card.?"

Ricardo debated on whether to ask why he was being stopped or should he wait for the officer's next move. Ricardo decided to wait. He passed his license and the registration card to the officer.

Officer Daniels. "The reason I stopped you is for speeding. "Where are you coming from?"

Ricardo responded by asking the officer, "Well how fast was I going?" Ricardo's instincts told him that he made a bad move. Putting the officer on the defensive was no way to end this matter quickly.

"Look officer I am sorry. I have had a couple of drinks with some friends in Tampa Bay and I am on my way home." Ricardo hoped that this bit of a confession would speed things along. If the officer indicated that Ricardo was going to get a speeding ticket, he would accept the ticket without the slightest objection or resistance.

Officer Daniels next remarks caused Ricardo to panic internally. "Sir, I am working a DUI traffic detail and I clocked you at 65 MPH in a 55 MPH zone for some time."

"Are you sure you only had a couple of drinks?"

Ricardo replied, "Yes, I am quite sure. This is ridiculous. Let's get this over with."

Surprised, Officer Daniels asked Ricardo, "What do you mean? I am going to give you a field sobriety test. Do you mind if I check the trunk of your vehicle for alcohol? Sir, please step out of your vehicle."

Ricardo viewed this as a bad situation getting worse. Uncle Sanchez had warned him to tighten up his security on transporting and transferring the cartel's money. There was no way Ricardo was going to let this officer search the trunk of his car and discover a half million dollars of Sanchez's money. Ricardo definitely did not have a death wish. Ricardo thought, a desperate situation called for desperate measures.

Ricardo had been sizing Officer Daniels up during the officer's questions. Ricardo practiced his martial arts on a regular basis and it would only take a moment to make a lightning offensive attack. This officer's uniform was very neat, he appeared to be Ricardo's age and in good physical condition. Ricardo did not like the odds of risking a physical assault on an officer without the deck being stacked in his favor of not losing.

Officer Daniels told Ricardo to step over to the right rear door of his Mercedes.

Ricardo was thinking about a second option that carried the risk of him being arrested on the spot for a criminal offense.

Officer Daniels put his hand on Ricardo's left shoulder and made a tapping movement. Ricardo's attention was diverted to his shoulder. Ricardo felt a slight chill on his right wrist and before he realized it, Officer Daniels had cuffed both of his writs together.

Ricardo knew that Officer Daniels was no ordinary street cop. At that moment he had no way of knowing the extent of Jack's special skills. Jack hung out with a select group of friends who considered themselves to be the best of the best.

Ricardo said, "Look officer, I really have to be somewhere and I am running late. For grins and giggles, would $10,000.00 in cash right now make this thing go away?"

Officer Daniels told Ricardo, "If you are serious, I am going to charge you with attempting to bribe an officer in addition to a DUI charge and impound your car if you fail the sobriety test."

Ricardo knew that he was in the mud up to his ankles so what could another step hurt. Ricardo said, " I mean no disrespect to you. I am not trying to bribe you. It is important that I make my business meeting and I thought $30,000.00 in cash right now, no questions asked, could make it happen."

Officer Daniels sensed that this guy was getting serious. Officer Daniels said jokingly, "Make it a $100,000.00 right now and you can walk."

Without flinching, Ricardo said, "OK, deal."

Officer Daniels felt nauseated in his stomach as he realized that Mr. Avilla was serious. He asked himself, "If this guy has $100,000.00 in the trunk of his car, what am I going to do?" Officer Daniels felt as if he was being pulled by an invisible force across a point of no return.

It was hard for him to believe that he was asking Ricardo, "OK, where is the money?"

Ricardo said, "Alright, we have a deal. The money is in a case in the trunk. I'll get it for you."

Officer Daniels said, "Hold on Slick. I may have been born at night, but it wasn't last night. I'll get it." Officer Daniels opened up the trunk and saw four very expensive leather bags. He didn't see the fifth bag in the rear of the trunk. Each bag contained $100,000.00 in US currency.

Ricardo was looking at Officer Daniels nervously.

Officer Daniels told Ricardo, "The situation has changed. I want half or the deals off. Final offer."

Ricardo said, "Be reasonable, man. This is not my money and believe me, you don't want to know. I can cover the $100,000.00. There is no way I can cover half."

Officer Daniels said, "Last chance. Its two bags or nothing. Your call."

Ricardo said, "I don't have a choice. I have to make that meeting. Take the two bags."

Ricardo arrived at his estate with virtually no memory of the drive after the officer removed the cuffs from his wrists. Ricardo knew that his uncle was going to kill both of them. Ricardo also knew that he had to tell Sanchez Avilla about the traffic stop sooner rather than later.

As Jack was driving away to secure his money, he realized that he had come face to face with the devil. Officer Daniels had surrendered to the devil's temptation and tarnished his badge of honor forever. In the span of a single significant moment, Officer Daniels made a regretful decision that would haunt him for the rest of his life.

Chapter TWO

Charles Drake was beaming as he reflected on the swearing in ceremony at his new office in south Florida. Drug Enforcement Agent (DEA) Charles Drake was chosen to head up the field office in south Florida because of his success as a team leader on eight previous assignments regarding the war on drugs. The officers on Drake's teams rose to the challenge of internal team competition to make the best field arrests. Agent in charge Drake encouraged his agents to make solid arrests every time. Big quality arrests made by our team will crush the drug dealers and outshine the other DEA teams that focus on small time quantity.

Agent in charge Drake by the authority of the United States Attorney General, swore in officers from various law enforcement agencies to serve on the south Florida drug task force on February 1, 2001.

The officers were:

Eugene Curtis, DEA

John Wiggins, Secret Service

Richard Edgar, Internal Revenue Service

Claude Whitman, Florida State Police/Vice Unit

Kate Johnson, Florida State Police/Vice Unit

Carl Beets, U.S. Customs Service

Janice Coates, Florida County Police Department

Angela Hernandez, DEA

Hector Ramos, ATF (Alcohol Tobacco & Firearms)

Edward Spaulding, FBI

Randall Holmes, Florida County Police Department

Isaac Fontaine, Florida County Police Vice Unit

Charles Drake knew that these officers had been thoroughly screened and were highly qualified to succeed at their mission. Each officer was comparable to a football player with an all pro-rating. They looked forward to playing the drug war super bowl against Sanchez Avilla and his Florida crew. He had a very good feeling about his new team.

The Washington DEA officials wanted the Florida drug task force to squeeze the Avilla cartel money houses and make Sanchez Avilla move his drug money through major money trails under DEA surveillance. Drake knew that the south Florida assignment was his chance to move up in the ranks of the DEA echelon. The top brass in Washington, D.C. expected Drakes' task force to hit the Avilla cartel with a crippling blow in America's war on drugs by thwarting Sanchez's latest money laundering scheme. They let Drake listen to taped conversations of Sanchez Avilla bragging to his banker, Harry Feldman. Sanchez planned to move his money through the Bank of America and have it transferred to the Bank of Nova Scotia.

Feldman used the code name of Mr. Clean. Feldman told Sanchez, "It will be no problem my old friend. I can make a clean route to the Cayman Islands without raising any eyebrows."

The Washington officials were pleased that Sanchez though of himself as the great chess player in Sanchez's game of wits to out-smart the law enforcement community. Big ears had recorded more of Sanchez's confidential conversation than he knew. Sanchez was quick to brag about his information network. Sanchez thought he was talking on a secure communication link when he spoke to instruct his nephew, Ricardo Avilla. Sanchez shared his plans to ship twenty million dollars through the American Express Bank International down to the Bahamas to close a big deal.

Chapter THREE

Randall Holmes, a Miami detective assigned to the drug task force, was Jack Daniel's connection to Miami's south beach crowd. Randall met Jack Daniels, Travis King, Gary Smith and John Barber at Central High school. The five young men became very good friends while competing on the Central High swim team against other high schools. They were fierce competitors in any sport activity. They lived to win. Randall was the swim team captain. Jack, Travis, Gary and John followed Randall's zeal for martial arts training, scuba diving and riding dirt bikes. Randall filled the role of natural leader for his four friends. The five friends formed a bond that was closer than many blood brothers.

After graduating from Central High, no one was surprised when the four friends followed Randall into military service to become parachutists. The men excelled at the rigorous training in jump school at Ft. Bragg, North Carolina. John Barber joined his father in the locksmith business after his honorable discharge from military service. Randall, Travis, Gary and Jack joined the police department and became police officers. Gary became an independent private investigator after three years of police service.

Randall met Sarah Leigh one afternoon during his rookie year on the police department when she drove by his marked police car at 85 MPH in a 65 MPH zone. Randall paced the speeding driver in her Mercedes convertible until he confirmed the speed of the vehicle. The driver identified herself as Sarah Leigh. He did not know that she was the daughter of Dallas Winston Leigh, a very wealthy and successful financial planner for some of the wealthiest families in Florida.

Officer Holmes asked Sarah, "Do you know how fast you were driving?"

Sarah replied, "Not really, I am late for a shopping appointment with some of my friends."

Officer Holmes began his safety speech about a driver's obligation to obey the law and respect the rights of other drivers. He said, "I would hate to get the call to investigate your accident. It would be a terrible waste of beauty."

Sarah looked at Officer Holmes and said, "Spare me the dramatics. Give me my ticket and I will be on my way, thank you."

Randall responded, "Thank you for telling me how to do my job. I am giving you a warning this time. I will give you a ticket the next time you pass me at 20 miles an hour over the speed limit."

Sarah smiled at Officer Holmes and said without sarcasm, "Thank you Officer Holmes for your professionalism. You look nice in your uniform. It fits very well on you. Which do you enjoy more, an opera or a stage musical production?

Randall was thoughtful for a moment before answering, "A stage production of course and don't forget the donuts. Why do you ask?" Are you trying to pick me up?"

Sarah shot back, "Well, you never know. Call me when you have a week end off. I will treat you to a show." She gave Officer Holmes her business card and a wink. Sarah drove off to her shopping engagement.

Randall called Sarah with the dates of his next weekend off. She totally surprised him with a trip to New York City on a private jet to see "Guys and Dolls". Their outing was a complete success. Sarah and Randall became very good friends. Randall and Sarah introduced her friends to his long time buddies. They arranged for Travis to meet Susan Gales. Jack was introduced to Kelly Francis. They set Gary up with Donna Jones. John Barber met several of Sarah' friends but he decided to keep his playboy image as a free wheeling single person. The five friends learned to live the life style of the rich and famous. It didn't take a long time for the five to be accepted as Sarah's friends and invited to endless dinner parties and social events of the financial elite in south beach Florida.

Chapter FOUR

Ricardo contacted his Uncle Sanchez and gave him a full account of the traffic stop by Officer Jack Daniels. Sanchez was Ricardo's father's younger brother. Ricardo's father, Ernesto Avilla was killed in a cartel operation eight years ago near Ricardo's hometown in Columbia. Since that time, Sanchez had been like a father to Ricardo.

Sanchez maintained a very strict rule regarding discipline and the cartel's business. He made no exceptions to his rule of trust. If someone made a mistake, Sanchez evaluated all of the circumstances involved in the incident. If he deemed the error to be an understandable human failure, Sanchez would forgive a first time mistake. If someone withheld information from Sanchez, that error might cost the person his life immediately. If the withheld information did not warrant Sanchez's death penalty, the person was put on the "never to be trusted again list." A sneeze at the wrong time by someone on the untrustworthy list usually resulted in a painful death.

Sanchez was not happy about the missing $200,000.00. He told Ricardo to get a message to the greedy cop. Officer Daniels had one week to return his money plus a $50,000.00 interest fee. If the officer missed the deadline by a minute, he and his family would be killed. Sanchez cautioned Ricardo about the task force's intelligence on their south Florida operations. Ricardo was to ensure that the money coming from Poncho Melendez's estate in Tampa Bay and the deposits from Jose Lopez's estate in Jacksonville arrived at the transfer point in Miami without further mishap. Ricardo knew that his uncle paid a great deal of money for his information network. Sanchez's ability to make strategic moves ahead of the law enforcement officials never ceased to amaze him. Sanchez was a master at the information chess game. Ricardo took good notes on his uncle's skills and planned to be just as successful when he took over the Avilla Cartel.

It was late afternoon on June 23, 2001 when Officer Jack Daniels received a call on his cell phone to contact the police department communications supervisor for an important message. Jack wondered what police business was so urgent that his precious day off on a Saturday afternoon was being interrupted. The communications supervisor gave Jack a cell phone number. He was instructed to call Harriet right away regarding a family emergency. Jack wondered what was going on and better yet, who was Harriet.

A female answered the phone when Jack called the mysterious number. She told Jack to listen very carefully. He would only hear the message once. She said, "The money you borrowed recently is due back to the lender one week from today. The interest is fifty. Your total due is 250. If you miss the deadline, your lender will pull the plug on you and your family." The phone connection was severed. Jack looked at the receiver of the pay phone in his hand and felt a wave of depression descending on his spirit. Jack knew that this latest development in his life would not make a welcomed dinner conversation for his four best friends at the beach party later that Saturday night.

Chapter FIVE

It was Susan Gales' turn to give the dinner party. Susan turned out to be more than a match for Travis. Susan's family's wealth dated back to the early discoveries of oil in Texas. Susan was a free spirited woman with a zest for life. She was sincerely dedicated to a daily scheduled physical workout that focused on different areas of the body each session. Susan spent the rest of her time as a socialite.

Susan had invited all of Travis' friends to her dinner party. She always enjoyed participating in the close affection the men shared with each other. Susan expected each of the five to attend her engagement and they did.

Randall, Travis, Gary and John noticed equally that something was troubling Jack. They let the evening progress and prepared themselves for Jack's eventual release of whatever it was on his mind. When the moment of privacy came in the poolroom away from their women friends, Jack's revelation was an eye popping and jaw dropping experience for the four friends.

As Jack relived the event of the Ricardo traffic stop during his recounting of the facts to his friends, they could see the torment on his face. Jack was in one hell of a mess. It seemed like an hour before anyone spoke. The threat from the cartel hit each of the four as if an actual death notification had been delivered. In reality, each of the men was so close they thought of themselves as brothers.

The friends watched Randall go through his slow boiling simmer. Randall always rose to a challenge. It was his nature. He was pissed to be sure at Jack for getting himself in such an idiotic predicament. Randall found it astounding that out of all the drug dealers or money couriers running around in Florida, his best friend would randomly stop the one kingpin that his drug task force was salivating at the jowls to take down. Randall could not believe that Ricardo Avilla had been so reckless.

The boldness of the cartel's death threat angered Randall more. Randall told his waiting friends, "A desperate situation calls for a desperate solution. Let's make a plan to pay the cartel the $250,000.00 back with cartel money. Randall understood the look of confusion on the faces of his friends. He began to share confidential information with his companions concerning the concentration of money at Ricardo's Miami estate. Randall's conservative estimate of a sure seven million dollars caused the four listeners to simultaneously emit a soft whistle.

Chapter SIX

The magic man was named Chester Wills at birth. He was raised by his mother, Charlotte Wills. She was a single parent. Charlotte became a successful real estate agent in Florida and worked her way to the position of selling estate home in the south Florida area. Miss Wills made regular hefty sales commissions from the business transactions on properties that sold for millions of dollars. Chester graduated from college with a degree in accounting. His mother wanted him to join her real estate firm.

Chester's first job after college was assistant entertainment host to the counseigere at the luxurious Belverdeire Hotel at south beach Florida. Chester enjoyed the praises given to him by the hotel's wealthy patrons. He was thrilled to be getting paid a handsome salary for making social connections for people with lots of money and little time to make connections for themselves. Chester followed his boss's philosophy which was founded on the principal, if money was no object then the sky was the limit.

Chester went into business for himself. Many of his clients described his efforts as work of art. "You made it happen like magic." Chester became known as the "magic man". Chester described his job as more exciting than the president of the United States. The Magic man changed his motto. He said, "I make fantasies come true. If you have the money, I can make it happen."

It became evident early in the planning stage to knock off Ricardo's estate that the friends would need some special equipment to achieve their goal. Randall decided to call in a favor from the Magic man. Randall helped one of the Magic man's clients avoid an embarrassing situation on their way to a social event. The client was grateful to Randall for his professional and tactful resolution of the incident. Randall's intervention saved the client valuable time and eliminated his need to call any one of four attorneys on standby for the client's beck and call twenty-four hours a day. The client expressed his appreciation to the Magic Man.

Randall called the Magic man. He said, "I need some very special equipment for a sensitive operation and time is of the essence."

The Magic man replied, "Randy, you know my rule."

Randall said, "This operation will pay for itself.

The Magic man. "Whatever you need, consider it done."

The Magic man had met Randall personally at three or four social events. He considered Randall as a very intelligent man. As the magic man listened to Randall's list, he had to upgrade his initial assessment of this likable young man. Randall's list proved that he was a serious thinker and obviously did not do any sleeping in his classes in school. The Magic man found the list entertaining. A couple of the items on the list made him laugh out loud.

Randall said, "I need a super wagon to meet four Cadillac Escalades at a very secure rendezvous. Randall cited the details regarding the location.

The Magic man said, "That's no problem." Getting specialty items on short notice increased the Magic man's value to his wealthy clients.

Randall continued, "I need ten super maxis."

Magic man. "I can get you ten of the improved version of the machine guns used by the military and police assault teams to rescue hostages." The Magic man thought that Randy was planning some type of a military operation. Anyone on the receiving end of a super maxi was in trouble if they didn't get an accurate and effective first round off first.

Randall said, " I will need six delivery systems of 'Sleeping beauty'.

The magic man whistled and said, " You have been talking to somebody in the C.I.A. There aren't many average Joes on the market with knowledge of that tranquillizer."

"Sleeping beauty" would make whatever Randy was planning look like a C.I.A. black bag operation

Randall said, " The last items on my list are two helicopters. I need helicopters and headsets with a special radio frequency and night vision equipment for twelve men. I want to put on a concert for canines with special treats.

The Magic man knew that Randy was planning for an encounter with guard dogs. The last item on Randall's list made the Magic man howl with laughter. The Magic man was able to complete many of his arrangements because of his friends in high places with political connections.

The Magic man did not know exactly what Randall was planning. He did know that the mission had not planned for the loss of one helicopter. Randy asked for two helicopters with night combat stealth capability, forward looking infrared(FLIR) sensors and the intergrated communication/navigation/identification avionics system. The Magic man called on one of his billionaire clients to supply the helicopters and cover the insurance of the aircraft. The Magic man figured that Randall had a lot on his mind.

CHAPTER SEVEN

The life support unit arrived at the front gate of Ricardo's estate on June 28, 2001 with emergency lights flashing. The emergency rescue squad truck was built as solid as a tank. The gate guard at the security booth had not received a call from the main house granting permission for an ambulance to enter the compound. The men on Ricardo's security team had been trained to pay attention to details and not take anything for granted. The guard took a closer look at the ambulance to describe the situation to Victor Cane, Ricardo's security chief. The guard noticed that the life support unit was large enough to transport more than two victims away from an emergency scene. The made its silent approach toward the estate's front gate just as the guard had made up his mind to call Victor about the two stealth helicopters flying over the garden area.

The front gate guard saw the two helicopters before he heard them. He watched the helicopters ascend into the dark sky. The mysterious machines came swooping into his view from the north section of the estate. The area of Ricardo's prized flower garden. The noise from the helicopters was more noticeable than the ambulance's approach but only slightly. Victor told the guard, "I want you to go on red alert." Victor engaged the red alert alarm for the rest of his team. Victor quickly confirmed that no one on the estate required medical attention. Ricardo asked Victor, "What in the blazes is going on around here?" Victor replied, "There's an ambulance at the front gate and I didn't call for it." Ricardo thought momentarily and stated, "I'll bet the task force is behind this. Uncle Sanchez said that a lot of coded information was being transmitted from the Miami office." Ricardo ordered Victor to check it out personally. Victor called the gate guard on his cell phone and said, "Keep that ambulance and everyone in it until I get there."

The guard at the gate assured Victor on the phone that he would keep the ambulance under close observation. As soon as he finished speaking to his boss, the guard felt the sting of the dart in his neck. The effects of "Sleeping beauty" put him down immediately. The chemically laced dart would make the guard sleep for at least four hours. Travis told the ambulance, "Turn on the concert music for the dogs." The special CD was the second phase of double agony for the guard dogs.

The helicopters had dropped several packets of filet mignon heavily saturated with the scent of a female dog in heat along the outer perimeter of the house. The ambulance driver played the music from the CD over the external public address system on the ambulance. The sound coming from the speaker could only be heard by the guard dogs and animals with a hearing range on the level of canines. The decimal level of the CD was higher than the wail of the speeding fire trucks en route to a call.

Victor stood on the front porch of the house and watched the dog handlers struggling to control their German shepherds. The dogs were howling in agony and dragging their handlers in different directions. The high pitched vibrations coming from the ambulance's speaker made the dogs ears ache to an unbearable degree. The dogs wanted to get away from the pain as badly as they driven to locate the scented packets of steaks. The pungent scent from the filet mignon scattered in the grass was pulling on the dogs like iron metal filings being drawn to a magnet.

In the midst of the confusion, the electric power at the estate went out. During the few moments of darkness Victor felt the sting of a dart on his neck. He was not able to focus his vision when he heard the emergency generator turn on. Victor was obliged to experience the rest of "Sleeping beauty". The expertly hidden sharpshooters had an easy time of picking off the four struggling dog handlers with "Sleeping beauty" darts. Each of the German shepherd dogs were put down with "Sleeping beauty" to keep the mission clean and uncomplicated.

The initial commotion by the ambulance at the front gate made Victor commit all of his security team to cover the perimeter of the estate house. Victor's red alert plan was designed to quickly set up a superior number of his men to contain, surround and overpower an attack on the estate.

Randall gave the helicopter pilots instructions to drop the entry team off. Randall assigned two members of the eight man team the task of deploying "Sleeping beauty" as a first option against any resistance encountered inside of the estate house if possible. All eight members of the team understood clearly that the members with the super maxis were to use immediate deadly force against any threat to a team member if "Sleeping beauty" could not stop the threat in time.

Ricardo was on the phone inside the estate's safe room describing the details of the attack to Sanchez when the plastic C-4 charge on the opposite side of the door exploded. The blast blew the door open. A security dead bolt lock attached to the inside of the door was hurled across the room through the air and struck Ricardo on the back of his head. Ricardo died before completing his sentence on the phone.

The entry team notified Randall that the estate was secure. Victor's entire security team had been overcome by "Sleeping beauty". Each man was cuffed at the wrists and ankles with flexi-cuffs. Randall told John, the locksmith, to work fast on the safe. Randall wanted to get out of the sticky situation as quickly as possible. Up to that point, everything went as planned. Randall was grateful to each volunteer on the mission. His prayers would be answered if he could pull this scheme off without losing a man.

Randall had almost decided at the last moment not to dial 911. Calling the police from the estate was a huge risk. The money from the walk in safe was loaded into the ambulance. The team carried out a lot of U.S. paper currency. Travis called Randall from the ambulance and said, "We are clear of the front gate now." Randall dialed 911 on Victor's cell phone. Randall did not say a word to the inquiring voice, "What is your emergency. Hello, hello. Is everything OK. What is your emergency." Randall left the line open with the phone next to Victor. Randall got on his helicopter and signaled for both pilots to take off. The helicopter lifted into the beautiful dark sky and disappeared into the night.

Chapter EIGHT

Charles Drake was awakened from a peaceful sleep by the ringing of his cell phone on June 28 at 11:45 PM.

Drake cleared his mind and said, "Hello, this is Drake."

The voice on the other end of the phone stated, "Agent Drake, this is Captain Marvin Jordan, the patrol watch commander. I am at the estate of Ricardo Avilla. We have a mess on our hands."

Drake was fully awake at the mention of Ricardo's name and asked, "What's going on out there?"

Jordan said, "I have a crime scene that looks like something out of a comic book. The chief of police told me to brief you right away. All of Ricardo's men were found drugged and tied up flexicuffs. Several guard dogs were drugged also. It looks like somebody used an explosive to gain access to the money room. The safe was opened and the suspects took all the paper currency and other valuables."

Drake listened to the watch commander in disbelief and asked, "Who reported the robbery?"

Capt. Jordan. "We don't know yet. A 911 call from a cell phone was made to the dispatch center.

Drake inquired, "Well where is Ricardo?"

Jordan. "Yeah, I was getting to that. He's here. Ricardo is dead. My two Identification Technicians are processing the scene now. One has finished shooting photos. I want him to assist with trying to recover fingerprints."

Drake pressed the captain for some clarity of the situation. He said, "Help me to see this picture. All of Ricardo's men were tied up. The guard dogs were drugged. Ricardo is there dead, right?"

Jordan. "Right."

Drake continued, "Did Ricardo make the call before he died?"

Jordan said, "No. The 911 call came from the scene. I hope you are sitting down because it gets worse. The caller used Victor Cane's cell to dial 911, the caller never said a word. The line was left open. The found was found next to Victor. The phone had been wiped clean. The ID tech couldn't even find Victor's prints on his phone.

Drake. "This is bad."

Jordan said, "Hold on. There were two scout cars in the area when the call was dispatched. The first unit arrived on the scene thirty five seconds after the call was broadcast to the patrol units. The second patrol officer marked out on the scene to back up the first officer nine seconds later."

Drake impatiently asked, "For Pete's sake man, what did they see?"

Jordan. "I told you it was worse. They didn't see anyone or anything on the way in. This looks like one of those black bag jobs. There are dots all over the place. We just haven't found any evidence to connect any of the dots together at this point."

Drake said, "Captain, do me a favor."

Jordan. "Name it."

Drake. "Tell me that I am dreaming. I am not really talking to you on my cell. I am stuck in the middle of a horrible nightmare."

Jordan. "Agent Drake, nothing would make me happier. I have to call Gregory Dixon, the homicide commander and go through this drill again for the fourth time tonight."

Chapter NINE

Charles Drake was not looking forward to his task force briefing on June 29. The information Captain Jordan told him last night would hit the member on the task force like a bowling strike. The details of the raid on Ricardo's estate would knock everybody down.

Drake began his meeting with his customary, "Good morning. You all should know that I was briefed on a situation by Captain Marvin Jordan, the patrol watch commander last night. The usual briefing room buzz began to subside. This morning I was trying to decide whether to fly to Washington, D.C. and serve myself as breakfast or wait for them to send for me. Either way, they are going to put my butt through the hopper. You can bet on that."

Agent in charge Drake had the complete attention of everyone in the room. Many of the officers looked at each other and asked with silent facial expressions, what is up?

Drake continued, "Ladies and gentlemen, something is rotten in the state of Denmark."

DEA Agent Eugene Curtis couldn't resist and said, "Agent Drake, that is a line from Shakespeare, I do believe. For a moment,

I thought you had some bad news to lay on us about our operation."

Florida Police Detective Randall Holmes joined the exchange and said, "Agent Drake, I do believe that line came from Shakespeare's 'Hamlet'."

DEA Agent Angela Hernandez said, "For the record, each of the distinguished gentlemen are correct."

Drake looked at his team and said, "I knew that this team was dynamite when I first met you. Outstanding. Now maybe someone can tell me who killed Ricardo Avilla and made off with approximately eight million dollars of the cartel's money last night.

A hushed silence filled the room. If a pin had fallen in the room next door, everyone in the task force briefing room would have heard it. Drake shared all of the information that Captain Jordan told him during the phone call. Drake had read the preliminary patrol reports from last night and he shared that information with the stunned group.

IRS Agent Claude Whitman said, "The timing of the raid on Ricardo's estate was incredible. We have been closely monitoring the activity at Poncho Melendez's Tampa Bay estate. Poncho just completed a sizeable transfer of money to Ricardo yesterday afternoon."

ATF Agent Hector Ramos added, "Yeah. We were prepared to track the money scheduled to move from Jose Lopez's Jacksonville Florida estate to Ricardo sometime today. You can bet that Lopez's money won't be moving before the 4th. This situation has ruined our plans to pull the plug on Ricardo's bank before the July 4th holiday."

Florida State Trooper Carl Beets said, "I have to agree with Agent in Charge Drake. There may be something rotten in Denmark. There is definitely something rotten in the state of Florida right now. How can these bandits pull off a job like this right now? We have been babysitting these turkeys for five months now. Someone has slipped in under our noses and made off with all of the gold. This doesn't smell good at all."

IRS Agent Richard Edgar chimed in, "Uncle Sam isn't going to come up short on this one. I am going to have the Miami office file confiscation papers on the remainder of the estate and all of the property on the grounds."

DEA Agent Drake. "Hold on Agent Edgar. Let's not jump the gun on this situation. We don't who these masked bandits are right now but that will not stop us from trying to catch them. Whoever they are, they must have gonads the size of grapefruits to rip off the cartel's money in the middle of our investigation."

FBI Agent Ed Spaulding said, "At least they kept the body bag count down to one. I doubt that it will be that low when Sanchez reacts to this intrusion on his turf."

Agent Drake. "Good point Ed. If the IRS moves on confiscating Sanchez's Miami property now, he may stall his operations at Tampa Bay and Jacksonville. A reaction like that would really set us back."

Secret Service Agent John Wiggins said, "Catching these masked bandits might be a bit of a challenge. There aren't many people who have the skills to pull off a stunt like this one. This job took some crafty planning. Agent Drake's comment about the grapefruits didn't go unnoticed. My guess would be that this crew has big brains as well. We have our work cut out for us now."

The other members of the drug task force shook their heads in agreement with Agent Wiggins' remarks.

Agent Drake said, "We need to keep an air tight watch on the other two money houses. Maybe we'll get lucky and catch the masked bandits in the act of taking the money."

CHAPTER TEN

Sanchez was getting ready to exit the steam room when Maria rushed to the door and told him to answer the phone.

Maria said, "Senor Sanchez, Ricardo wants you on the phone right away."

Sanchez rushed to his office to talk on his private line.

Ricardo unleashed a rush of information as soon as Sanchez answered the phone. Sanchez found himself getting a little annoyed as he listened to the information Ricardo was rattling off. Ricardo was usually calm and managed stressful situations well. Sanchez had personally supervised his nephew's training in the cartel's business. Sanchez had big plans for Ricardo's rise in the business. Ricardo was cut off in mid sentence. Sanchez noticed that he was gripping the telephone in his hand tighter and tighter as he listened to the silence on the other end. Without warning the line went dead.

Sanchez was trying to figure out what was happening at his nephew's money house in Miami when the muffled noise of an explosion came across his telephone. Ricardo sounded excited when Sanchez picked up the telephone. Ricardo told Sanchez that several helicopters were flying around the estate grounds and armed men dressed in black uniforms were storming the main house. Sanchez was waiting for Ricardo to complete the first wave of information about the activities at the estate when he heard the explosion in the background.

Sanchez called his second lieutenant in Tampa Bay, Poncho Melendez.

Sanchez. "I don't know what is going on at Ricardo's estate. I want you to check it out immediately and tell Ricardo to call me."

Poncho told his boss, "I am on it right away."

Poncho ordered Raphael Semidey, his security chief, "Get my car and a couple of the boys. We are going to see Ricardo."

Sanchez was a no nonsense leader. He was known for blowing up at unpredictable moments over the smallest distractions. Sanchez had fired bullets at several of his men for talking in hushed whispers while he was talking on the phone. Sanchez was not trying to hit any of his men but he did not let them know that. His men knew that Sanchez was an excellent shot. There were many men in dusty graves in Columbia that were proof of his willingness to shoot a man.

Poncho knew that Sanchez's reaction to the news of his nephew's death was going to be violent. He tried to prepare himself for a most unpleasant phone conversation with the cartel's head man.

Sanchez asked Poncho, "What did you just say?'

Poncho repeated, "I hate to be the one to tell you that Ricardo is dead." He was killed during a robbery at the estate. All of his men were detained for questioning at police headquarters."

Sanchez was coldly silent for several moments on the other end of the phone. He, said, "I want you to find out everything that you can as soon as you can and report back to me. I will make arrangements to get Victor here."

Poncho knew that Sanchez was not receptive to changing his mind at any time. If someone had a better suggestion about Sanchez's decision on an issue, it had to be put to Sanchez very diplomatically.

Poncho suggested, "Senor Sanchez, I know this is a difficult time for you. Let me pick Victor up. I can get the information you want and handle things on this end."

Sanchez. "OK Poncho, you handle this mess for right now. Report back to me as soon as you can."

Samuel Taylor, the lawyer hired by Poncho, did not have a lot to say to Victor Cane as they drove to the International House of Pancakes about ten miles from Poncho's estate. The 24 hour restaurant was a good public location for Victor to be seen getting out of the lawyer's car. Victor was summoned to a waiting limousine as Samuel drove off with only a nod of good-bye.

Victor did not know what to expect from the interview with his boyhood friend, Poncho. He thought back on their childhood in Colombia. The five of them, Ricardo, Poncho, Jose Lopez, Victor Cane and Raphael Semidey, growing up were as thick as thieves. Victor knew that Sanchez chose Poncho as his second person in command in Florida because of Poncho's serious attitude about the cartel's business.

Victor would have been sweating a lot more if he had known Sanchez's first reaction to the raid on the Miami estate. Sanchez wanted to make a strong example of Victor. He wanted his men reminded of his intolerance for failures under his command. Victor would have been grateful for Poncho's success in calming Sanchez's rage.

Poncho updated Sanchez on the information he had regarding the raid on Sanchez's money house. Poncho said, "The thieves took approximately eight million dollars in cash."

Sanchez told Poncho, "I want my money back. The men who took my money are dead men. They just don't know it yet. I want you to hire some investigators to gather any and all information on this operation. I want you to start with that greedy cop, Jack Daniels. I have a feeling he might be behind my money being stolen. Put Victor on the phone."

Victor told Sanchez, "I am really sorry about Ricardo. He was like a brother to me."

Sanchez. "Victor, I have known you since you were a little kid. I accept your statement of sorry for my nephew. He was like a son to me rather than a nephew. What's done is done. I want you to do me a favor."

Victor said gratefully, "Anything Senor Sanchez, just name it."

Sanchez said, " I want you to help Poncho and Jose straighten out the mess up there in Florida. I want you to get a handle on things in the trenches for me. Can I count on you."

Victor felt like he had been punched in the stomach. He never saw it coming.

Victor responded, "Of course, Senor Sanchez. It will be my pleasure."

Sanchez. "Let me speak to Poncho."

Victor had been demoted to the drug side of Sanchez's Florida operation. Any portion of the cartel business carried certain risks. Victor enjoyed a luxurious life style on the money security and shipment side of the business working with Ricardo. Sanchez's success in the drug business was based on keeping the drug operations and money collection for the drugs separate. Sanchez's customers paid for their drugs up front. Sanchez's clients are guaranteed delivery of their orders. If a shipment is confiscated because of law enforcement intervention, the cartel sends a replacement order at no additional charge to the customer.

Victor had been content working his way to the top of the organization in Ricardo's shadow. Ricardo was a blood relative of the head man. Victor relied on his skills as a survivor in the trenches of the drug game. Now he was starting at square one again. Victor thought, well at least I am alive.

Chapter ELEVEN

The members inside the cartel, in the know, referred to him as the snake man. Sanchez used him more frequently for big jobs because he was deadlier than the six deadliest snakes in the world. Victims bitten by the Taipan, King Cobra, Krait, Puff Adder, the saw scaled viper and Russell's viper rarely recovered from the bites to live. Striker's victims never survived his attacks.

Striker was his code name. Striker came from a secret society that produced assassins as their way of life. Killer for hire was their professional calling. Striker started his training when he was five years old in the martial art of Ninjutsu. He became a skilled swordsman and expert in throwing knives, shurikens (Ninja throwing stars), the use of pistols, rifles, the bow and arrow and poisons.

Striker's first professional contract hit at the young age of 22 as a hired killer was a successful mission. He completed a number of additional successful assassinations before his reputation as a high dollar player was established. Striker worked alone and his hitting average was 1,000. He had the heart and conscious of a statute when he was on a job. If the devil needed a hit man, Striker would have been the devil's choice for the job.

Striker became a millionaire after six years in the business. Striker set a retirement goal when he was selected by the cartel to be on the million dollars a hit assassins list. Striker wanted to retire within ten years. He planned was to make the greatest amount of money in the shortest possible time and retire at the top of his game. Striker wanted to retire with guaranteed financial freedom and enjoy a life of luxury. He knew that only a few of the very good assassins retired before they were killed or captured on an assignment.

All of Striker's contract contacts were controlled by a family of contract guarantors. The cartel and any client had to submit a contract offer through four levels of security to retain the services of Striker. No one outside of the family knew who Striker was or what he looked like. The four levels of security (the circuit) were established before Striker was born. The family circuit has always consisted of blood relatives. A client had to be referred to the first level of the circuit to post a contract.

A fee of $100,000.00 and details of the contract is relayed to the second circuit. Each level of the circuit deducts a non-returnable fee of $25,000.00 and forwards the contract information to the next level. The contract information is posted by the fourth level on an electronic information network that is reviewed daily by contract agents. When an agent accepted a contract, a code name and a bank account number was given to the fourth circuit. The client would be given instructions by the first circuit to deposit the entire contract amount in a specific bank into the account of the agent's code name.

Striker wasted no time accepting the latest contract proposal listed by the cartel. The contract listed five targets. The two million dollar bonus money paid up front made it possible for Striker to think about an immediate retirement after the elimination of the fifth target. Sanchez's representative deposited the seven million dollars in Striker's coded Swiss bank account. Striker transferred the money to his secret retirement account in the Cayman Islands. He made up his mind to permanently disappear as soon as this job was completed.

Chapter TWELVE

Drake knew the situation of the staff on the task force had to be handled deftly. He could not afford to let the morale of the team deteriorate because of mistrust amongst the agents. Drake called his supervisor, Anthony Wallace, and requested a huge favor.

Agent Drake convinced Supervisor Wallace that putting a new agent from another department was the best way to do damage control for the morale of the team. Agent Drake requested that FBI Agent Andrew Hart be assigned to his task force. DEA Agent Wallace realized that time was of the essence. Agent Wallace used his political contacts to make the transfer of FBI Agent from Washington, D.C. to Florida happen.

Andrew had spent five years as a patrol officer on the Metropolitan Police Department in Chicago, Illinois. He attended classes at night and earned a bachelor's degree in accounting. The FBI was fortunate to get Andrew during a recruiting drive for minorities and people skilled in speaking a foreign language. Andrew was an African-American who spoke excellent Spanish. He was a current Black Belt Karate champion. Andrew graduated as the number one student in his FBI academy class.

Agent Drake introduced FBI Agent Andrew Hart to his drug task force team as the agent with the responsibility of identifying the masked bandits as soon as possible.

Agent Drake. "I want everyone on the team to be assured that I have complete confidence in all of you. I would be surprised and disappointed in you, if you did not suspect that possibly someone on the team compromised the integrity of our investigation. Agent Hart has also been given the task check out that angle.

I know personally that Agent Hart is an excellent investigator. We have worked together on previous task force missions. If anyone can find out the identities of the individuals involved in the Ricardo killing with the least amount of disruption to our team, I know that Andrew Hart is that person.

DEA Agent Angela Hernandez said, "Well Agent Drake, if Andrew works as good as he looks, he has my vote.

The other members in the room laughed at Angela's remarks.

Agent Hart said, "The investigator in the purple blouse is prettier that the regal hue of the garment that she has on and she has the voice of an angel."

ATF Agent Hector Ramos said, "Well that takes the mystery out of who Angela will vote for. He works fast. I must warn you Senor Hart. Angela was known as P & D in defensive tactics."

Agent Hart asked, "P & D. Let me guess, pretty and daring."

Agent Ramos said, "That's close but it means pretty and deadly. She is a Kung Fu master. Watch out for her kick."

Florida County Officer Janice Coates said, "Not so fast. Andrew has got my vote too. Andrew looks as if he can take care of himself in a scrap."

Agent Hart looked at Investigator Coates, winked and said, " I know a little Karate. I started when I was young and it helped with my growing up in the "Hood."

Florida County Officer Randall Holmes said, "I look forward to working with Agent Hart. I may be able to pick up some of that F.B.I charm for my game. A fellow struts in here and picks up quick votes of confidence from most of the best looking women on the team. The F.B.I has got it going on."

The briefing room erupted in laughter.

Agent Drake. "Agent Hart will work closely with each of you for a few hours at a time."

Florida State Trooper Whitman said, "That's cool with me. I will volunteer to work with Mr. Internals Affairs first. Then I can focus on my investigation. We don't want to be left, looking like a bunch of amateurs."

Agent Hart said, "I do appreciate the cooperation. Just call me Andrew or Andy if you prefer."

Officer Randall Holmes. "Andy works for me." He walked over to Andy and gave him a soul brother handshake. Randall topped it off with bumping his chest against Andy's chest and placing one arm around his back.

Agent Hart responded to Randall's chest move like a skilled dance partner and he placed one arm around Randall's back.

Andy said, "Homeboy, look at you. Getting down brother-man."

Randall shot back, "My man."

Angela walked over to the two men and stated, " I want to get on this welcoming session." She turned to Andy and said, "Let me give you a hug."

Agent Drake was pleased with Agent Hart's warm acceptance by the group as a new member.

CHAPTER THIRTEEN

It was March 3, 2002, time for Striker to put his plan in motion.
Striker was aware of Donna's Gem on the horizon long before
anyone on the shore. Striker felt Donna's Gem before he saw the
boat through his binoculars as the Gem gracefully approached
her slip at the dock. Striker was parked in a discreet location that
attracted no attention. His stakeout was as patient as the bald eagle
soaring on a powerful air current looking for its next meal. Just
as the eagle plummets from the sky to snare its victim, Striker's
descent on the unsuspecting couple would be as devastating.

Donna Jones was thoroughly pleased with her afternoon with
Gary. Gary Smith, private investigator, made Donna feel special
when he was separated from his friends and devoted all of his
attention on her.

Donna said, "We have been like two ships passing through a
fog in the night. I barely get a glimpse of you it seems."

Gary responded, "Yes my darling, I know. As soon as I finish
this interview in Tampa Bay tomorrow, I will give my client a writ-
ten report on my investigation. We will take that Alaskan cruise
that we have put off so many times."

Donna. "The timing is perfect. I will make a quick turn around in London and fly back to you just as fast as a jet can bring me. I can think of nothing better that being on a ship with you in Alaska for five days. Just the two of us."

Gary. "Honey, what about the other people on the cruise? Don't they count?"

Donna. "Not in my book, baby. I only have eyes for you. I won't even know that they are there."

Donna's chauffeur met her at the dock. He drove Donna to the Miami airport to catch her plane for London, England after she said good-bye to Gary.

Gary waved one last time as he watched the limousine drive away with his sweetheart. Gary loved spending time with this woman. Donna was the breath of fresh air that gave meaning to his life. He thought, man am I lucky. I have four friends who are better than any brothers most people have as relatives. I have a beautiful woman that treats me like a king. This is the life. I have found Heaven on earth.

Striker didn't know what was going through Gary's mind as he watched Gary from the rear of the Cadillac Escalade. The darkened windows on the vehicle kept anyone from seeing Striker. Striker thought, it would not be long now. Truly, the clock was ticking.

Gary had no idea that he was targeted in the dark angel's sight. Gary first noticed the presence of death when he felt the shift of the Gem's weight. The Gem had been doing her usual gentle rock while tied to her dock slip. Gary had spent many hours on the Gem with Donna. In the calm waters, he knew the Gem's graceful dance in his sleep almost better that the Gem's owner, Donna.

Gary was wide awake when death climbed aboard. There was no doubt in Gary's mind. Someone had come aboard the Gem.

For a split second Gary thought about getting his gun. He dismissed the idea in another second. Gary climbed the stairs to the upper deck to investigate. Gary felt the presence of Striker before he saw the assassin as he neared the top stair.

Striker selected the darkest corner adjacent to the stair door of the sleeping quarters. He became a part of the black shadow cast by the position of the Gem at the dock. Striker knew that Gary was looking for him.

Striker also knew that Gary would make the same mistake of so many hunters before him in the wild. The number one rule for hunters on a lion hunt is to be prepared to meet a lion face to face when hunting for one. In the jungle or the environment of the prey, sometimes the hunted becomes the hunter.

Gary felt the chill of fear. It had been a month since Gary worked out with Travis at the martial arts studio. Gary had bested Travis three out of five practice matches. Of the five friends, Randall was the best martial arts fighter and Travis was number two. Gary would give either of the two a run for their money during some training sessions.

At the moment Gary felt the dread of looking for the boogey man. He could feel of the presence of the devil in the darkness. Gary knew that he was there. He felt himself being drawn to the shadow to take a peek anyway.

Gary turned the corner and peered into the face of the dark outline in the darkest part of the shadow. He was startled to see that a person was actually there.

Striker blew the poisonous dust into Gary's surprised face. Gary gasped at the speed of the attack and reacted by throwing a Karate blow designed to crush an opponent's Adam's apple. When he gasped, the poisonous particles were drawn into Gary's airway.

Striker blocked Gary's blow, grabbed his extended arm and spun Gary around. The poison had an immediate effect on Gary. Thousands of bright colorful lights and dots exploded in front of his eyes. He felt himself being spun around.

The pressure Striker exerted on Gary's neck and chest was incredible. Gary knew that he was in a sleeper hold. The strength of the demon was mind boggling. Gary could not move at all. Gary's mind was barely able to recognize the sensation of a peaceful sleep taking control of his body. His mind was not able to process the fact that Gary would not awake from this sleep. Striker released Gary's soul into the darkness of the night.

Another promise was fulfilled. Death came like a silent thief in the night. The date and time was completely unknown the victim.

The news of Gary's death on March 4, took everyone by surprise. The preliminary police investigation revealed that Gary suffered a heart attack. The medical examiner's report was expected to answer some of the puzzling questions pertaining to the timing of his death. At the age of 41, Gary was in excellent physical condition. He was rarely ill. There were no witnesses on Donna's Gem when he died. There were no obvious signs of trauma on Gary's body.

John Barber, the locksmith, was affected deeply by Gary's death. John was the free wheel in the circle of friends. Donna received a lot of moral support from Sarah Leigh, Susan Gales and Kelly Francis. John spent time with Randall, Travis and Jack to talk about their grief. John started going to the Pleasure Den on a regular basis and would drink for a couple of hours alone.

On March 15, John had been in the Pleasure Den for about an hour. He was unaware of elderly looking gentleman who had John under surveillance. John got up from his table and started toward the rest room. No one in the room noticed the elderly gentleman when left his seat and began shadowing John toward the rest room. The Pleasure Den was a private upscale club in Miami. A disturbance in the Pleasure Den usually meant that a patron needed assistance with walking to his limousine or on the rare occasion to a cab.

The rest room was empty when John entered. He walked to the nearest stall and entered. John was closing the door when he felt some resistance from the other side. The door was pulled open and John looked into the face of an elderly looking gentleman. Before he could say excuse me, the white powdery substance from the man's mouth was enveloping John's nostrils. John had no way of knowing that his gasp was almost identical to Gary's reaction to the messenger of death. It is possible that John would tell Gary about the bright colorful lights and dots that he saw. John slumped to the floor of the rest room stall. He was beyond medical assistance two minutes later. Three minutes after inhaling the secret Ninja poisonous powder, John died.

The preliminary police report indicated that John was discovered deceased in the rest room stall by a patron of the Pleasure Den. Witnesses in the club did not recall anything unusual happening in the club prior to the last patron going in to use the rest room. There were no signs of trauma on John's body. It appeared that another 41 year old male in perfect physical condition had a sudden fatal heart attack.

Sarah, Susan, Donna and Kelly were disturbed and depressed at the latest news of John's death. The autopsy report listed the cause of Gary's death as cardiac arrest of unknown origin. The preliminary police investigation of John's death was leaning the same way.

Randall, Travis and Jack knew that the two deaths so close together were more than coincidental. The three men had been sent a cold calculated warning from Sanchez. It had been almost nine months since the death of Ricardo and the theft of Sanchez's money. The snake unleashed by Sanchez had reared it's ugly head. The three private investigators hired by Poncho had compiled a wealth of personal information on the south beach friends. Randall and his friends had very good reasons for being troubled.

CHAPTER FOURTEEN

Jack called Kelly at work on March 29. "Ms. Francis, would you mind being taken to dinner this evening by a handsome young man who is crazy about you."

Kelly. "I don't know any crazy young men and I certainly don't date strangers."

Jack. "My dear, I stand humbly corrected. Would you give this man the pleasure of your company at dinner tonight and I am crazy about you."

Kelly said, "Well Mr. Daniels if you put it that way, how can I refuse such an attractive offer?"

Jack. "Ah, you can't refuse; so, don't. What time shall I pick you up?"

Kelly. "Jack, can you pick me up at my place at 7 PM?"

Jack. "Dearest, your wish is my command. I'll see you at 7 PM."

Kelly. "OK, Jack. I love you. Bye."

Jack. "I love you too, sweetheart. Bye."

On March 28, the previous Thursday, a tall elderly looking man with white hair told George Skinner that he wanted an accident staged.

George Skinner had a team of scam artists operating in the south Florida area who were cleaning out the insurance companies with fake claims of personal injuries and property damage claims.

George. "How did you find out about me?"

Striker. "That's not important as long as the money is good. I am not the law. If I were you would be looking at some serious jail time. Let's cut to the chase."

George. "I am all ears."

Striker. "I want you to use my Hummer to stage an accident with the man in the picture. It is important that I know exactly where he is for at least thirty minutes."

George. "What is so important about this guy?"

Striker. "Shut up and listen. It's what he has in his apartment that's important to me. I will only have one chance to get my merchandize and there can absolutely, positively be no slip ups. There is no second chance in this high stakes poker deal."

George. "What are your terms?"

Striker. "I will show you how to use this tracking monitor. His 2002 Jaguar has a bug attached. This monitor shows exactly where the Jaguar within the transmitting range. You can follow him from the gym where he works out tomorrow. Stage the accident and call me on my cell phone."

George. "Is that it?"

Striker. "It should be a piece of cake."

George. "What kind of incentive are we talking here?"

Striker. "I will give you $50,000.00 in cash right now. I will give $50,000.00 in cash tomorrow evening when you return my Hummer and the tracking monitor."

George said, "OK, when do you tell me the name of the joker I have to kill for the $100,000.00."

Striker opened his case and dumped $50,000.00 on George's desk "If one of those presidents tell you to kill somebody. You do it. All I want you to do is stage the accident and call me." If you do anything extra, I don't pay overtime."

George looked at the money and verified that the bills were good. "We have a deal."

Striker. "There is one small detail. Get a professional driver to drive the Hummer. Hold the damage down to a bear minimum if possible. That is my final request."

George. "You can trust me. I will set it up."

Striker. "I don't trust anybody. I double check myself. If you take my money and don't deliver, you can trust me. I will kill you."

George felt a chill as the elderly man walked out of his office. He was glad he didn't make a play to get some of the apartment break-in action. George, being the con man that he was refused to let the temptation of not completing his end of the bargain to enter his mind.

George assigned Jerry Redford the job of driving the Hummer. He told Junebug to drive the 1985 Buick, the jam car.

George followed Jack's Jaguar from the gym onto Forest Park Boulevard driving north toward Hamilton Ave. George told Jerry to get in position with the Hummer.

Jack saw the Hummer when it pulled up on the left side of his Jaguar. The Hummer had a very noticeable gold color. Jack was driving at 45 MPH and his mind was on getting home to prepare for his date with Kelly. Jack's defensive driving skills automatically kicked in when he saw the Hummer accelerate and cut in on his lane.

Jack said out loud, "What is that guy's problem?" Jack jammed on the brakes of the Jaguar.

George told Junebug, "OK, jam the Jaguar from behind."

Junebug. "I got it boss. No problem."

Jerry stopped the Hummer on the left front fender of the Jaguar without doing much damage to either vehicle. Jerry stayed in behind the wheel in the Hummer.

Jack noticed the driver behind the Jaguar acting strange when he automatically checked his rear view for an escape route. Jack was amazed that the Hummer pulled in front of his for no apparent reason and his front airbag did not inflate.

The '85 Buick was jammed against the right rear fender of Jack's Jaguar. The driver stayed in the Buick holding his head.

Jack stepped out of his car to look at the damage.

George had stopped on the side of the road behind the Buick. He dialed the cell phone number given to him by the elderly man. "We got him. He won't be going anywhere for awhile."

Striker. "Excellent work. I will see you at the meeting place with the rest of your money."

George could not contain the grin on his face as he thought about the other $50,000.00.

Jack wondered why neither driver had gotten out of the vehicles. He decided to check on the man in the back of the Jaguar first. Jack knew that he was going to be late for his date when he saw the right rear quarter panel of the Jaguar pressed against the tire.

Jack walked over to the driver in the Buick and asked, "Buddy are you alright?"

The man in the Buick was holding his neck with both hands. It dawned on Jack that this seemed like one of those insurance scams recently mentioned on the news.

The man in the Buick said, "I do feel a little shaken up right now but I will be OK."

Jack started walking toward the Hummer. He was at the back of the driver's door of the Jaguar when George saw the black Cadillac Escalade barreling down on Jack.

Jack did not see or hear the large sport utility vehicle (SUV). George watched the SUV as it ran over Jack. Jack did not have a chance to escape. George threw up his breakfast on the steering wheel of his tan Lexus.

The big black SUV ran over Jack and never slowed down. The Cadillac made a right turn onto Hamilton Ave. and sped out of sight.

George didn't know who Jack was but he knew a scam when he saw one.

In the excitement George did not see the traffic helicopter overhead taking pictures of the incident. The helicopter lifted higher in the air and began following the black Cadillac SUV.

George shouted, "Junebug get that Buick out of here. Take it to Harold's right now."

George drove up to the Hummer. "Jerry get out of that car. Move your ass, damn you. Let's get out of here."

George called Harold. "Get a bay ready for me. We're coming in hot."

Harold. "I have got you covered. Bring it home." Harold thought, this might be a busy day.

George followed Junebug in the Buick to Harold's auto repair (chop) shop. George noticed a Rib Shack delivery van driving away from Harold's shop as he followed Junebug toward Harold. Harold directed the '85 Buick to an open bay.

George asked Harold, "What are you celebrating?"

Harold. "A customer ordered lunch for the entire shop. I love doing business with intelligent businessmen. This guy was first class all the way. Not only did he pay in cash up front. He treated us to a free lunch." Harold laughed.

George started to ask Harold more about the customer but he had a pressing situation to deal with. "Harold, take this baby apart right now. There is no time to waste."

George looked out of the garage and noticed the high flying helicopter for the first time. The aircraft seemed very interested in some activity on the ground near Harold's auto shop.

George stayed with Harold inside of the bay until the cutting crew reduced the pieces of the vehicle into car parts not recognizable as parts from the '85 green Buick. George watched Jerry as he destroyed the tracking monitor with an acetylene torch.

George knew that he would not see the $50,000.00 promised by the elderly man. He hoped that he would never see the mysterious man again.

Everyone in the chop shop heard the wail of sirens as police cars descended on Harold's auto repair shop. In a matter of moments police officers were everywhere.

Harold said, "Look at that parade. You'd think that a cop has been killed."

George became so faint he almost passed out. He started dry heaving. There was nothing left in his stomach to come up.

Chapter FIFTEEN

Striker had a lot of work to do on Wednesday, March 28. He found Harold's auto repair shop without difficulty. As usual Poncho's information was very reliable.

Striker. "Harold, I was referred to you by a business associate. I was told that you can be counted on to be discreet."

Harold. "True that, my man. Discretion is the name of my game."

Striker. "I want to drop off a vehicle for an emergency paint job tomorrow. It is imperative that the vehicle receive immediate attention."

Harold. "We may have a problem. I have promised delivery on two cars tomorrow. I can't make you any promise at this time."

Striker. "I am a business man. Time is money. I am not asking you for a favor. I want to hire you to do a job. Are you a business man?"

Harold. "Time is money. I like that. You have my attention. I'd like to think that I have more time than money. I am down for trading some time for more money."

Striker. "I'll pay you $50,000.00 for a paint job on a large vehicle."

Harold. "We are talking about paying for my time up front, right."

Striker opened his case and put $50,000.00 in U.S. currency on Harold's desk.

Harold was visibly reminded about the saying that money indeed talks.

Striker. "I take your noticeable silence as a yes."

Harold. "Yes sir. Yes. Keep talking. I didn't want to interrupt you."

Striker. "I may need storage of the vehicle for a week or two. I will give you a deposit of $25,000.00 of which you can deduct your daily storage rate." Striker put another $25,000.00. in cash on the desk.

Harold could hear his heart beating. He started to laugh out loud but the seriousness of the man sitting in front of him stifled the thought.

Harold composed himself and said, "Might there be anything else?"

Striker. "I might need a ride from here to my associate's office if his driver get delayed or tied up. I'll pay $100.00 for the ride and leave a $400.00 deposit of good faith. Striker gave Harold another $500.00.

Harold. " Is that all?"

Striker. "No. I would like to buy lunch for you and your staff tomorrow. I will make the arrangements. I will call you before I come."

Harold. "Mister, you can call me anytime. I'll see you tomorrow. Don't worry about the ride to the office. I will drive you myself if I have to."

Striker drove to the Rib Shack on Hamilton Ave. about two minutes away from Harold's auto repair. He approached the manager on duty and read his name tag.

Striker. "Roscoe, I need your help. I am planning a special birthday lunch party for my niece, Barbara Chapman, at her new job. By the way, how much do you make in tips a day?"

Roscoe. "You must have me confused with the hired help. I am the manager. The only thing I get is to handle customer complaints."

Striker gave Roscoe a one hundred dollar bill. Striker gave Roscoe the number of complete rib dinners with desserts, sodas and extra sides that customers normally order for office parties.

Striker. "I will call you when I want the order sent over. It is very important that you have a driver standing by. I would prefer to hire someone from your evening shift to wait for my call. I would not have to worry about your day driver being delayed or tied up for whatever reason."

Roscoe. "Your niece must be some kind of special. I should have had an uncle like you."

Striker. "I love her like a daughter. I would give her the world if I could."

Striker gave Roscoe five one hundred dollar bill.

Striker. "$100.00 is for the driver to stand by. I will give him or her another $200.00 when I arrive at Harold's auto repair shop.

The driver must be at the shop when I get there. The other $400.00 is for you to make sure that I have a driver."

Roscoe. "Are you paying for the order up front?"

Striker. "Of course. I would not have it any other way."

Roscoe. "I will have my evening driver Floyd standing by. I will let him drive my Dodge caravan to make the delivery."

Striker. "Do you think I could borrow one of your rib uniform shirts? Barbara will get a kick out of seeing me as a delivery person carrying rib dinners.

Roscoe started laughing. He said, "No problem, man. That should be a sight to see you walking in with rib dinners. I love it."

Striker. "Roscoe, you are a good man. Let me give you your tip up front." Striker gave Roscoe five one hundred dollar bills.

Roscoe checked the money for authenticity when the business man left the Rib Shack. The money was good.

Thursday, March 29 Striker had no idea that a news traffic helicopter caught his dirty deed on camera. The helicopter followed the black SUV to Harold's auto repair shop. The cameraman got footage of the SUV going into an open bay door. Someone inside closed the door after Cadillac Escalade drove inside.

The helicopter pilot said, "Get a shot of that gold vehicle behind the green car. Those cars were at the accident scene."

Cameraman. "I told Gregg to call the police. It is a lucky thing for us that we were in the area. This should make the evening news exciting."

Pilot. "Something is up. The green car drove into the same garage with the black SUV."

Cameraman. "Wow, I saw that. I have it on film. Unbelievable. This hot."

The pilot and the cameraman saw a minivan leave Harold's auto shop. The overhead camera shot of the gold Lexus and the green Buick captured the minivan as it passed the two vehicles traveling in the opposite direction.

Striker saw George driving behind the green Buick when the two vehicles drove past Floyd. George did not see Striker in the back seat of the minivan.

Striker asked, "Can you drop me off at the bus stop?"

Floyd. "Roscoe told me to take you wherever you want to go. The bus stop it is."

Striker gave Floyd $300.00 in cash.

Floyd thanked Striker and drove off. Floyd thought about Roscoe's comment. That dude must have money to burn. I am glad that he shot a little money my way. Floyd smiled as he drove back to the Rib Shack. He found Striker's generosity satisfying as well.

Striker called a cab on his cell phone. The cab picked him up and took Striker in the opposite direction of the police activity on Forest Park Blvd.

Chapter SIXTEEN

The hit and run death of Officer Jack Daniels set off alarms all over the Police Department. The police chief was all over the commander of the homicide division regarding recent coincidental deaths. The chief wanted to know why an FBI Agent Hart working on the drug task force made the connection between Gary Smith, a private investigator and a former police officer on the Department and John Barber, a lock and key businessman when his homicide investigators had not.

The Chief said, "Somebody had better get to the bottom of these so called coincidental deaths, put some case jackets together and make a solid arrest or arrests if need be."

FBI Agent Hart made a shocking discovery while research-ing background information on Gary Smith and John Barber. Both men joined the U.S. Army with three other friends, Randall Holmes, Travis King and Jack Daniels after the five young men graduated from Central High School. The five friends went to Ft. Bragg in North Carolina for paratrooper training after their Army basic training.

Agent Hart. "Agent Drake, I want you to be the first one to hear it from me. I think Detective Holmes may be tied in with the ghost burglars that everyone has been searching for."

DEA Agent Drake. "Andrew, I appreciate the information. I have been analyzing the reports by the investigators on the task force and other units in the Police Department. We have a lot of information about the cartel's illegal activities. I haven't seen didley squat to link Randall and his friends to the burglary at Sanchez's money house.

You can be sure that if Sanchez has information on Detective Holmes, it will just be a matter of time before that serpent strikes.

Agent Hart. "My investigation into the alibis of every member on the task force on the night of the burglary revealed that everyone has a solid alibi.

I could not find any illegal activity that involved the five friends. The Internal Affairs investigators moan and groan when they are asked to check out an allegation of wrong doing by Jack, Travis or Randall.

The only thing the men seem to be guilty of is enjoying the good life. They have wealthy girl friends who don't seem to mind sharing the wealth with a group of good looking, fun loving men."

DEA Agent Drake. "You are preaching to the choir son. I have been over that same ground myself. The deaths of three of the five friends does add a new wrinkle to the picture. Somebody knows something. The only thing I know right now is that the dead men aren't talking. Not even a whisper."

Agent Hart. "Give it time Agent in charge Drake. Give it time. Time has a tendency to tell all in due time."

Travis was headed to the Pleasure Den to meet an unknown female, who claimed to have information relating to the deaths of Gary, John and Jack. Travis' police specialty was investigating bad checks and fraud cases. Jack's death made investigating leads regarding his case a higher priority for the department.

Travis was grieving internally over the deaths of his friends more than he would admit it to himself. Under different circumstances, he would have shared this lead with Detective Holmes.

Randall told Travis, "I think Andrew and Agent in charge Drake suspect that we are involved in the Ricardo money rip off. They can't prove anything but they are suspicious.

I know why Drake selected FBI Agent Hart to join the task force. That guy doesn't miss anything."

Travis. "Why do you say that?"

Randall. "Let me put it another way. He pays attention to everything. Andrew remembers more about personal conversations in the briefing room than the people who made the statements. His analytical view of information in police reports is amazing. I was tempted to ask Andrew if he worked on jig saw puzzles for a hobby."

Travis. "Why didn't you?"

Randall. "I was afraid that he might say yes."

Travis did not want to subject Randall to any unnecessary heat from Drake or Hart.

The female informant told Travis that she would meet him at a booth at 2 PM at the Pleasure Den. Travis' police instincts warned him of a set-up.

Travis parked two blocks away from the Pleasure Den at 1200 noon. He called a cab on his cell phone.

Travis. "I am looking for something special for my girlfriend. Drive so that you will be able to turn when I tell you."

Cabdriver. "My time is your time, the meter's running. Tell me when."

Travis told the cab driver to turn at various intersections. Travis made mental notes of the buildings, windows and vehicles parked on the street. It did not take the cabdriver long to see that they were carefully circling and surveying a specific area.

Travis paid his cab bill and started walking toward the Pleasure Den. He was thinking about that gut feeling he had right after agreeing to participate in the raid on Sanchez's money house.

Travis didn't hear a thing. He felt a jolt. As he laid on the ground, Travis felt the gradual chill creeping over his body. Travis knew that his end was near.

Images from his childhood began flashing across his mind. Travis wondered, does God review the information that is stored in your mind when you stand before him.

Travis remembered a television medical program about brain surgery. The brain surgeon explained that the brain records everything that a person sees, hears, feels and even smells. He described the brain as a vastly misunderstood miracle.

The surgeon recalled a follow-up experiment on a surgery patient. The anesthetized patient was able to recall every word spoken by everyone on the medical team during the patient's operation.

Travis had intended to get on the path for salvation and accept Jesus Christ as his personal Savior. Travis recalled saying numerous times that he would get around to it one day. Travis lifted his hand toward the sky and weakly thought, please Lord Jesus, I beg your forgiveness for my sins.

I have made some serious mistakes over the course of my life. I tried to help the good people when I could as a police officer most of the time. I should have done a better job of being my brother's keeper. Dear Lord I.

Striker had snuffed out the life of another victim. He was nearing his retirement goal. The count was four down and one to go.

Some of the people around the fallen victim heard the rifle shot but no one knew where the shot came from.

Chapter SEVENTEEN

Striker would make an air tight plan for his attack that contained three levels of contingencies for "What ifs". After a final review of his plan Striker would not think about his victim until the morning of the day slated for the victim's death. Last night was different. It was the first time Striker could remember that he had a dream about his next target.

Striker devised a plan that would exploit Randall's crucial weakness, Sarah Leigh. He planned to eliminate Detective Holmes without mercy or delay.

Striker did not have any trouble getting into Sarah's luxury villa. He was prepared to deal with her alarm security system. The open sliding glass door on the second floor balcony made it a breeze for stealthy assassin to get in.

Sarah was so surprised when she saw Striker in her bedroom, she almost passed out from nausea. Striker pounced on Sarah with three quick strides and placed his sword against her neck. The cold steel blade made Sarah shiver immediately. The sharpness of the blade was pushing her to the point of panic.

Striker said, "Follow my instructions exactly and you will live. Cross me in the slightest manner and you will die."

Sarah called Randall on his cell phone. When his phone rang, Randall saw Sarah's home number on his caller screen.

Randall cheerfully answered, "Hello, baby. What's up?"

Sarah said, "Randy, I am at my villa."

Sarah's phone went dead.

Randall called the number back. Someone picked up the phone. Randall heard only silence.

Randall looked over at Andrew's desk and said, "I have got a problem that I need to let you know about. Are you up for a helicopter ride on short notice?"

Andrew winked at Randall and said, "They don't call me Action Andy for nothing. I was born ready. Let's go."

Striker concealed his Mercedes Benz behind Sarah's garage without attracting any attention. He did not want Randall to see his car and know he was probably inside the house. Striker was counting on Randall to approach the house with caution every step of the way until he found Sarah.

Striker drugged Sarah and hid her in the guest bedroom closet. He used a special blend of muscle relaxants that would make Sarah sleep for a minimum of three hours.

Striker felt that something was amiss a full minute before he heard the sound of the helicopter in the distance. Striker's senses were attuned to anything out of the ordinary when he was in any phase of a job.

Striker had not planned for Randall's arrival in a helicopter. He decided to adjust his attack plan and confront Randall in another section of the house.

Striker saw Randall and FBI Agent Hart when they repelled from the helicopter and quickly disappeared on the far side of the villa.

Striker had done his research well on Detective Holmes. He was keenly aware of Randall's martial arts ability. Striker did not know about the FBI man. It didn't matter. Striker knew that he was the best hand to hand combat fighter in the business. He was able to make a kill in seconds.

triker decided to confront the two law enforcement officers on the first floor. He hid behind a column in the foyer near Sarah's library. He was certain that the officers would follow police training. They would make a cautious courtesy check of the first floor. The two men would expect Striker to be either upstairs or down on the recreation level.

Striker listened as the two men began converging on his position at an angle. As the men closed in on his deadly accurate range of ten feet, Striker thought for a moment. This was going to be too easy.

Striker began making a mental adjustment to his escape plan. Randall's use of a helicopter surprised the assassin. He had a few surprises in the specially equipped Mercedes. The occupants in the helicopter would never know what hit them.

Striker waited for Randall to advance three more feet. He was listening to each advancing cautious step. Striker knew that Randall would be a dead man within three minutes after he broke the invisible plane ten feet from Striker. At ten feet, he could hit a target dead center every time with his lethal shuriken.

Randall was two feet away from being able to see striker. His senses told him that striker was very, very near. Randall took another step.

Striker shifted his upper body just enough to launch the deadly projectile. The shuriken's target was Randall's neck.

Randall detected the movement of Striker from the corner of his eye and bent his knees slightly as he turned a slight fraction toward Striker.

Striker was certain of Randall's death because he got a good release on his deadly projectile. He shifted his stance to launch a similar attack on Andrew.

The poison laced shuriken struck Randall on his left cheek instead of the carotid artery on his neck as planned by Striker. Randall's lightning quick reaction to Striker's attack made a world of difference in the outcome.

The devastation and pain from the razor sharp edge of the shuriken was immediate. The impact of the weapon made Randall raise his right gun hand slightly and fire a single shot. The bullet hit a metal Roman statute that was adjacent to the wall behind Striker.

Striker knew that Andrew was at the ten feet mark. He was a fraction of a second from releasing his second Ninja throwing star when Randall's bullet ricocheted off the statute and hit Striker in his right knee. The bullet's impact and pain caused Striker to give up his position of cover as he threw his second shuriken at Andrew.

Andrew was three steps away from Striker when Randall's gun went off. Andrew immediately flexed downward at his knees. He saw Striker for a fraction of a second as the upper portion of his torso emerged from behind the column and launched the deadly star. Andrew fired his pistol twice in quick succession at a point on Striker's mask that covered his nose.

In that instant Andrew felt the whiz of an object as it zipped through the air where his head had been. Andrew's first bullet hit its mark squarely. The second bullet was not necessary. Striker died as instantly as many of his victims when they were ambushed.

Striker was thinking about his plan to attack the helicopter for his escape when everything went black.

Andrew rushed to the side of his fallen friend. Andrew used his handkerchief to stem the flow of blood from Randall's cheek. Randall was conscious but the poison was draining his strength by the second.

Andrew said, "Hold on buddy, we'll get you on the helicopter and have you in that hospital in no time."

Randall looked into the eyes of the FBI agent that he had come to admire and gave Andrew a weak smile. Randall was too tired and drowsy to try to speak.

Once air borne, the helicopter would have Randall at the hospital's emergency room in three minutes.

As the numbness was gradually creeping all over his body, Randall knew in his heart that he was not going to make it this time. In his mind he knew that he could only cross his fingers and hope for a merciful verdict on the other side. Randall shared the fate of his four friends. Time had run out for him too.

Andrew looked at his friend with a growing sense of loss. Sarah shared the same helicopter ride to the hospital with her love for medical attention. Andrew saw the calm appearance of sleep on Sarah's face and the relaxed mask of death on Randy's face.

Andrew's heart began to ache as he thought about the pain Sarah had suffered during the past month. The medical staff at the hospital would help her recover from the effects of the drugs Striker gave her. Then Sarah would have to say farewell to her love. Her knight in shining armor had been called home. It was Sarah's turn to receive the support from her South Beach girl friends during her time of grief that she generously gave to them earlier.

Andrew thought about the details Randall shared with him regarding the cartel burglary. Jack Daniel's moment of weakness to the devil's temptation cost the lives of five good men. Andrew knew that if he were one of the four friends, he would have made the same decision to try to save his brother. Yes the devil racked up a victory on this one. Sanchez paid a lot of money to bring about so much pain and misery to a group of innocent fun lov-ing people. Andrew felt the familiar sensation of grief engulfing his spirit. He also experienced that slow burn that made Randall Holmes rise to a challenge.

The devil was due interest on his investment. Sanchez was the giant in the Avilla drug cartel. Andrew would be his David on the law enforcement side. DEA Agent Charles Drake and FBI Agent Hart worked well together on bringing down previous drug bar-ons. Andrew would focus his sights on Sanchez Avilla's Cartel. The war on drugs was just heating up.

THE END

ISBN 141202480-3